The Empathetic Soldier

This book shows the contribution that empathy can and should make to the proper conduct of war.

US Army doctrine identifies empathy as an essential trait in soldiers; despite this endorsement from senior leaders, empathy's role in the military profession remains obscure. The notion of soldiers empathetically considering others, especially enemies, strikes many as counter to the nature of soldiering. Additionally, confusion caused by differing definitions of empathy often leads to its complete dismissal. This work clarifies the concept by considering recent philosophical, psychological, and neuroscientific research, and demonstrates the relevance of empathy to the tactical and strategic demands of war. Empathy amplifies soldiers' understanding of human actors in an operational environment, enables soldiers' critical and creative thinking, and improves their overall intentions, planning, and assessments of a war's progress. While empathy can make soldiers more susceptible to the psychic wound of moral injury, it also helps prevent and overcome this injury. Instead of dismissing it, soldiers should assimilate empathy into their moral frameworks.

This book will be of much interest to students of the ethics of war, psychology, and military studies generally.

Kevin R. Cutright is an Academy Professor in the Department of English and Philosophy at the US Military Academy, West Point. His operational experiences have driven his interest in the ethics of military planning and conduct, as well as the moral psychology of soldiers.

War, Conflict and Ethics

Series Editors:
Michael L. Gross
University of Haifa
and
James Pattison
University of Manchester

Ethical judgments are relevant to all phases of protracted violent conflict and inter-state war. Before, during, and after the tumult, martial forces are guided, in part, by their sense of morality for assessing whether an action is (morally) right or wrong, an event has good and/or bad consequences, and an individual (or group) is inherently virtuous or evil. This new book series focuses on the morality of decisions by military and political leaders to engage in violence and the normative underpinnings of military strategy and tactics in the prosecution of the war.

Ethics and Military Strategy in the 21st Century
Moving Beyond Clausewitz
George Lucas

The Moral Status of Combatants
A New Theory of Just War
Michael Skerker

Distributing the Harm of Just Wars
In Defence of an Egalitarian Baseline
Sara Van Goozen

Moral Injury and Soldiers in Conflict
Political Practices and Public Perceptions
Tine Molendijk

The Empathetic Soldier
Kevin R. Cutright

For more information about this series, please visit: https://www.routledge.com/War-Conflict-and-Ethics/book-series/WCE

The Empathetic Soldier

Kevin R. Cutright

Routledge
Taylor & Francis Group

LONDON AND NEW YORK

First published 2022
by Routledge
4 Park Square, Milton Park, Abingdon, Oxon OX14 4RN

and by Routledge
605 Third Avenue, New York, NY 10158

Routledge is an imprint of the Taylor & Francis Group, an informa business

British Library Cataloguing-in-Publication Data
A catalogue record for this book is available from the British Library

Library of Congress Cataloging-in-Publication Data
A catalog record has been requested for this book

ISBN: 978-1-032-16341-3 (hbk)
ISBN: 978-1-032-16343-7 (pbk)
ISBN: 978-1-003-24813-2 (ebk)

DOI: 10.4324/9781003248132

Typeset in Times New Roman
by codeMantra

Nassim Nicholas Taleb popularized the term black swan *for an utterly unpredictable and improbable event of high consequence. That's Pamela. Out of nowhere came the astonishing shock of her beauty, spirit, intelligence, and companionship.*

To my black swan.

Contents

Acknowledgements

I am thankful for the communities in which this work has grown:

Saint Louis University – the mentors, teachers, and friends: Eleonore Stump, Jeffrey Bishop, Tobias Winright, Theodore Vitali, Colleen McCluskey, Dan Haybron, John Greco, Scott Berman, George Terzis, Naomi Eilan, Elizabeth Fricker, Jon McGinnis, Eric Wiland, Kathryn Lindeman, Luis Pinto de Sa, Matthew Shea, Audra Goodnight, James Kintz, Minghe Li, Sean Hagerty, Jason Chen, Yiling Zhou, Alexandra Romanyshyn, Alan Misenheimer, Barbara Manning, Heidi Moore, Adrienne McCarthy, Jamie Hendrix, and Tina Godar.

US Army School of Advanced Military Studies – those who encouraged running with the original idea: Alice Butler-Smith, Andrew Shoffner, Christopher Marsh, and Matthew Schmidt.

Past and Present Colleagues in the Department of English and Philosophy, US Military Academy – those who kept the trains of thought from running off the track (at least, catastrophically): Clark Rice, Richard Schoonhoven, Graham Parsons, Steve Woodside, Scott Parsons, Steve DiLorenzo, Nathan Pfaff, and Will MacKenzie.

Colleagues-at-large – proving the social endeavor that philosophy is: Pauline Shanks Kaurin, Andrew Cohen, and Mark Wilson.

Family and friends – for collaboration and moral support: Barbara Cutright, Judy Parker, Bob Cutright, Mark Hill, Caitlin Coe, Scott Hill, Mark Anthony, Tyson Anthony, Essam Altuhafi, Monte Hoover, Don Williamson, and Dave Mead.

My bride – Pamela Cutright, who makes marriage a beautiful community of two.

Many thanks to the editorial team at Routledge, particularly Andrew Humphrys. And to Anna Clarkson for such earnest support early on.

This book is derived in part from an article published in the *International Journal of Philosophical Studies*, 30 April 2019, © 2019 Informa UK Limited, trading as Taylor & Francis Group, available online: https://doi.org/10.1080/09672559.2019.1608059.

1 An Empathetic Soldier?

While mentioned sporadically in military theory and even official US Army doctrine, empathy's role in the military profession remains obscure, partly because it sits uneasily with military culture. Its presence in doctrine means it has been endorsed by senior leaders, but many in the ranks struggle with how it is to be integrated with other, more clearly martial, virtues. Add to this struggle the confusion over what empathy actually is, and it quickly becomes easier to dismiss it or keep it at the fringes of professional consideration. It is my intent to clarify the concept of empathy in light of recent philosophical, psychological, and neuroscientific research, and then to show the relevance of empathy to the tactical and strategic demands of war. Empathy amplifies soldiers' understanding of the human actors in an operational environment, enables soldiers' critical and creative thinking, and improves their overall intentions, their planning, and their assessments of a war's progress.[1] In military vernacular, empathy proves vital for the "cognitive dimension of warfare."[2] These benefits derive from the nature of empathy as an experiential understanding of another's mental states, such as emotions, beliefs, perspectives, or intentions, and the integration of this knowledge into further deliberation.

My argument rests primarily on empathy's epistemic nature in understanding other persons, but this understanding obviously carries over to important moral judgments. To examine empathy's moral impact, I will consider it in light of principles within the just war tradition. This tradition divides the morality of war into three main categories: the morality of initiating war (labeled *jus ad bellum*, or "justice of war"), the morality of conducting war (labeled *jus in bello*, or "justice in war"), and the morality of concluding war (*jus post bellum*, or "justice after war").[3] These distinctions reflect the separate moral evaluation of war's ends and means. (I agree with Brian Orend, among others, who notes the "robust connection" that remains

DOI: 10.4324/9781003248132-1

between them.)[4] Despite the significant contribution that empathy can and should make to the judgments of *jus ad bellum* and *jus post bellum*, I intend to focus on the second category of *jus in bello*, which presumably offers the most intractable obstacles to empathy's relevance. The notion of soldiers empathetically considering others, especially enemies, strikes many as counterintuitive, counterproductive, and possibly counter to the very nature of soldiering. Thus, I will devote the present effort to this center of gravity.

The traditional principles of *jus in bello* are right intention, discrimination, and proportionality. Right intention refers to the goal of establishing a "just and lasting peace," which a morally justified war is meant to secure.[5] Accordingly, one finds this principle emphasized under *jus ad bellum* as a correction for political leaders who may have a justified cause for war, but want to use that cause merely as a screen for other purposes. Many just war theorists, especially earlier ones, also include right intention under *jus in bello* as a similar correction for soldiers. The second principle of discrimination, more exclusively in the soldier's domain, involves the restriction of lethal force to enemy combatants, respecting and preserving the well-being of noncombatants and striving "to avoid killing them incidentally."[6] Finally, the third principle of proportionality entails restricting force to only that which is necessary to secure legitimate military objectives. It rules out "purposeless or wanton violence," the "excessive harm" that is all too common in war.[7]

Beyond these traditional principles of *jus in bello*, I will follow the lead of James Dubik in expanding the topics considered under this category. In an important contribution to the just war tradition, Dubik distinguishes between war-*fighting* and war-*waging* to more fully describe the activities within war.[8] War-fighting refers to the activities that occur on the battlefield itself, particularly the wielding of lethal force against the enemy through the weaponry at hand. With war-waging, Dubik means the activities that precede, direct, coordinate, and sustain the war-fighting on the battlefield – the comprehensive management of a war and not merely the specific battlefield actions that occur within it. "Fighting a war concerns the tactical dimension of war's conduct; waging a war concerns the conduct of war's strategic dimension."[9] He argues that the just war discourse has focused exclusively on moral principles relevant to war-fighting, with no moral analysis of war-waging. Yet, Dubik observes that "decisions made at the strategic level…either increase or decrease the probability of success in war, increase or decrease war's duration, increase or decrease the probability that lives will be well used or wasted."[10] Dubik seeks to correct this omission by examining...

> the responsibilities that senior political and military leaders have at the strategic level. These are the responsibilities to establish proper war aims, strategies, policies, and campaigns and set in place processes for cross-government department coordination as well as coordination among allies, methods to adjudicate conflicts in priorities, and procedures to ensure departmental support for important war policies meant to achieve sufficient unity of effort and coherence in action throughout the war.[11]

Leaders, I will argue, fulfill both war-fighting and war-waging responsibilities better with an empathetic understanding of others. While motivated by recent experiences in Iraq and Afghanistan, empathy remains relevant beyond population-centered counterinsurgencies. Empathy may play a larger role in counterinsurgencies, but I am not ready to admit that its role disappears in conventional conflicts. Empathy offers both moral and practical benefits across the full spectrum of military operations, which become clearer as it is better understood. Furthermore, like any other character trait, empathy depends upon, and must be integrated with, other virtues, capacities, or skills for its proper function. It is not a panacea to cure the ills of modern warfare, nor a silver bullet to neutralize future threats on the horizon, but its incorporation instead of dismissal is crucial.

In the end, the problem of empathy's relevance for the military profession involves two sources of confusion: a conceptual confusion regarding the nature of empathy and a parallel confusion regarding the nature of soldiering. The first confusion is the focus of Chapter 2, where I examine empathy and the type of understanding that it provides. I tackle the second confusion by splitting it into two aspects, comprising Chapters 3 and 4. In Chapter 3, I examine the foundational purpose of soldiering and take up the concern that empathy would seem to make soldiers more hesitant to use force in combat, especially lethal force. In a justified war, this reticence would impede the legitimate exercise of force for some moral good. Empathy, then, would seem to make soldiers less competent.

Might it also make soldiers more susceptible to moral injury? This concern is the second aspect taken up in Chapter 4. Moral injury is a psychic trauma involving debilitating guilt or grief that has received an increasing amount of attention from those assisting veterans of recent wars. The term is largely attributed to Jonathan Shay in his 1994 work *Achilles in Vietnam: Combat Trauma and the Undoing of Character.*[12] As Shay's title implies, only the term is new – the phenomenon is as old as war. In arguing for soldiers to be empathetic, I am arguing that soldiers keep the humanity of their enemies, noncombatants, and comrades at the fore. This attitude may make the likelihood of guilt and grief higher and their intensity greater. Promoting empathy, then, may produce soldiers who are more vulnerable to moral injury.

I offer a detailed introduction to moral injury below, but first I want to summarize the limited consideration of empathy and war in the scholarship of either topic.

Sparse Discussion of Empathy and War

Empathy and war are rarely connected in their respective literatures, largely due to the presumption that empathy is not relevant, and probably detrimental, to the employment of military power. One important exception is the work of feminist scholars focused on theories of international relations.[13] Christine Sylvester defines empathy as "the ability or willingness to enter into the feeling or spirit of something and appreciate it full…to hear what…[others] say and be transformed in part by our appreciation of their stories."[14] Empathy, according to these theorists, can help correct a hyper-rationalistic approach to state relations that ignores the influence of emotion. It can improve states' understandings of each other and move past the entrenched realist assumption of a zero-sum game in the international scene. Empathy can enable states to "understand their strategic interests as sometimes complementary rather than always at odds."[15] These benefits of empathy seem right, but they all reside at the level of grand strategy and *jus ad bellum* concerns. Feminist theorists provide far less detail on the role of empathy in the issues of *jus in bello*. When it is mentioned, the claim is that empathy promotes solidarity and personalizes the suffering of the enemy.[16] Such impacts are what fuel the concerns of others that empathy makes soldiers less willing to perform their difficult duties and less competent at them. I take up the accuracy of these impacts and these concerns in Chapter 3.

Two military ethicists offer important, though brief, exceptions to the general absence of empathy in *jus in bello* discussions. In the second edition of her book, *The Code of the Warrior,*

Shannon French notes "the importance of not silencing conscience or dampening natural empathy."[17] She provides two battlefield illustrations. Upon witnessing American soldiers kill a Vietnamese boy at My Lai, Hugh Thompson...

> landed his helicopter and ordered his crew to take up firing positions against their fellow Americans to stop the killing and allow for the evacuation of survivors. When asked why he took such drastic action, Thompson later explained, "You see, I had a little boy that same age back home in the States. And I was thinking, 'What if that were my son?'"[18]

French's second illustration involves Sir Hugh Dowding, a British pilot in World War I, who was shocked to watch a downed German pilot and crewman "shot while climbing out of their wrecked plane by ground troops."[19] Dowding insisted on dropping the Germans' personal effects behind enemy lines "with a note saying exactly where their bodies were buried."[20]

These two examples highlight the beneficial impact of empathy that I aim to reinforce and clarify. Thompson's empathy enabled him to interrupt the infamous massacre at My Lai. The benefit of Dowding's empathy is more circumspect and controversial, in that it motivated him to take on great personal risk not for military victory but to maintain a sense of honor. This honor, however, can prove vital to a veteran's well-being.

Nancy Sherman is the second ethicist who includes empathy in her consideration of war's conduct.[21] More specifically, she focuses on the mental and emotional struggles that some soldiers face in the aftermath of war, especially the moral injury mentioned above. Sherman notes that empathy is crucial for caregivers to help soldiers cope. Perhaps more importantly and innovatively, Sherman suggests that soldiers need to exercise self-empathy and to grant themselves "mercy and understanding" to recover "a sense of lost goodness."[22] In her most recent work, Sherman explains Stoic notions of social connection that lean on empathy.[23] Sherman seeks to correct the contemporary distortion of Stoic wisdom with its overly individualistic quality. It is through connection that the Stoics believe we can stay grounded; Sherman applies this belief to veterans needing to reintegrate into society.

One of the few military tacticians who has explicitly noted empathy's relevance to war's conduct is retired major general Robert Scales. In a short essay of 2006, Scales notes that future conflicts will continue to require the kind of cultural knowledge that most soldiers have lacked in the counterinsurgencies of Iraq and Afghanistan:

> The military of the future must be able to go to war with enough cultural knowledge to thrive in an alien environment. Empathy will become a weapon. Soldiers must gain the ability to move comfortably among alien cultures, to establish trust and cement relationships...[24]

I do not contest the implication that empathy is required for trust-building and relationships, but I am not ready to conflate empathy with cultural knowledge. Having participated in the US Army's efforts at increasing cultural knowledge among soldiers, and having watched many try to apply this knowledge during deployments to Iraq, I have become convinced that greater cultural knowledge contributed only minimally to building relationships. What was more important was how soldiers engaged Iraqis, whether equipped with that knowledge or not. Empathy, in short, involves an interpersonal understanding that goes beyond the factual knowledge of cultural traditions, regional history, and social customs. Cultural knowledge can aid in empathetically understanding another, but it cannot replace the insights and attitude that empathy provides. I return to this issue at the end of Chapter 2 and in Chapter 3.

More recently, Matt Waldman has also argued that empathy has a significant role to play in resolving violent international conflict.[25] In his critique of the intervention in Afghanistan beginning in 2001, Waldman argues that what was missing in US policy-making...

> was empathy: imagining or simulating another's experience and perspective, in order to better understand them. Empathy, in this sense, is rational and cognitive...a tool for understanding the way another person thinks, feels or perceives. It enables us to comprehend another's mindset, driving emotions or outlook, without requiring us to share the other's thoughts, feelings and perceptions, or, indeed, approve of them. An empathic approach involves the assimilation of diverse information, including social, historical and psychological details, and a conscious effort to see the world through that person's eyes. Thus, it serves the first demand of strategy: know your enemy.[26]

It is this claim of improved understanding gained through empathy that I want to secure. I think Waldman and the feminist theorists above are right, in that empathy has more to contribute to national security than is commonly grasped. However, there remains the question of how empathy can be reconciled with the lethal duties of soldiers. In addition, rooting empathy in imagination or simulation is contested among relevant scholars. Dan Zahavi, for instance, argues that imaginative perspective-taking is not empathy but a different form of social understanding. He claims that empathy should be "understood as a perceptually based and theoretically unmediated experience of the other."[27] In this view, empathy is not the projection of a speculated mental state onto another, but the direct perception of another's mental state, similar in some ways to sense perception. Imagining or mentally simulating another's circumstances may help in understanding their emotions, beliefs, and intentions, but Zahavi argues that this effort should not eclipse the genuine empathetic moment of one person *experiencing* another – a moment of direct awareness, not conjecture. Overall, Zahavi notes that social understanding...

> is a collection of different abilities that interact in various ways, and that we need multiple complementary accounts in order to cover the variety of abilities, skills, and strategies that we draw on and employ in order to understand and make sense of others.[28]

The pressing question is whether we ought to use the term "empathy" for Waldman's "tool for understanding" or whether it is best regarded as one of these other "abilities, skills, and strategies."

The answer to this question would help to clarify the US Army's doctrinal references to empathy, which serve as one of the only other attempts at a connection between empathy and war. Empathy is explicitly mentioned in doctrinal manuals on advising foreign security personnel and leadership.[29] Furthermore, empathy is implicit in other doctrinal manuals on counterinsurgency, intelligence analysis, operational planning, and information operations (the military term referring to influencing or disrupting the decision-making of adversaries).[30]

I have not examined all US Army doctrine across the organization's history, but empathy seems to have first appeared in the 2006 revision of counterinsurgency doctrine resulting from the struggles in Iraq and Afghanistan.[31] While the term is not in the latest update of 2014, it is worth examining the 2006 language to illustrate the rationale for its appearance and its unsettled nature. The writers encourage an empathetic understanding of others: "Leaders feel the pulse of the local populace, understand their motivations, and care about what they want and need. Genuine compassion and empathy for the populace provide an effective weapon against insurgents."[32] The terms "compassion" and "empathy" appear basically synonymous, especially with the directive to "care about" the wants and needs of the local populace. Furthermore, after noting the imperative for cultural knowledge in counterinsurgency operations, the manual urges "commanders, planners, and small-unit leaders...to avoid imposing their ideals of normalcy on a foreign cultural problem."[33] The imposition of foreign ideals may be improper and generate great resistance among the local populace, but the adoption of local ideals can be just as problematic. The manual seems to insist that soldiers adopt and tacitly agree with the local ideals, when, in fact, soldiers should only be asked to understand them. Both of these aspects of empathy – empathy as distinct from compassion and empathy as entailing understanding but not agreement – are overlooked in this 2006 doctrine, probably because the academic literature on empathy reflects similar confusions. These confusions may explain the absence of the term in the 2014 update.

The Army's doctrine on advising foreign security forces underscores empathy's significance. Empathy is listed as one of many personality traits to consider when assigning military personnel as advisors. In its description of empathy, the manual acknowledges the difficulty of empathy as a concept, yet its vital role in building relationships:

> Empathy can be defined as identifying with and understanding another's situation, feelings, perspectives, and motives. Cross cultural empathy is tough to accomplish and harder to explain, but understanding it and overcoming [one's] own cultural biases is key to the success of an advisor mission. Understanding other human beings and their motivations allows for the development of honest relationships, which is a critical factor of success. In most cultures, the way to begin understanding another person's feelings and experiences is by understanding the other's narrative. The narrative is a collective group's identity as an interpretation of ancient history and recent collective experiences. Delving into the narrative, understanding the context, and how it affects people is the beginning of empathy.[34]

This reference to empathy shares the same two concerns found in the counterinsurgency doctrine above. Presumably, "identifying with" another refers to something shared, perhaps camaraderie or purpose. To identify with another is, at some level, to agree on something. Second, it implies a kind of caring in which the empathizer takes on the other's well-being or projects as important to herself. To identify with another is to have a vested interest in that other, a personal stake in what happens to him. Yet, linking empathy with both agreement and care obscures the notion of understanding the other, which is, I intend to argue, the essence of empathy (see Chapter 2).

This advising doctrine also connects empathy to narrative, reflecting the position of some empathy theorists. Peter Goldie defines empathy as "a process or procedure by which a person centrally imagines the narrative (the thoughts, feelings, and emotions) of another person."[35] As highlighted above, however, Zahavi and others maintain that empathy does not involve imaginative projection, but consists of a direct awareness of another's mental states akin to perception. Grasping a person's narrative (which, itself, requires further clarification) may very well contribute to understanding that person, but the question remains whether this effort is a moment of empathy or something else.

The Army's leadership doctrine contains the second explicit reference to empathy. It lists empathy as a character attribute, stating that empathy is the "ability to identify with and enter into another person's feelings and emotions, enabling clearer communications and better guidance."[36] It expands on this notion with the following:

> Army leaders show empathy when they genuinely relate to another person's situation, motives, or feelings. Empathy does not mean sympathy for another, but a realization that leads to a deeper understanding. Empathy allows the leader to anticipate what others are experiencing and feeling and gives insight to how decisions or actions affect them. Leaders extend empathy to others in both their leader and follower roles. Leaders with a strong tendency for empathy can apply it to understand people at a deeper level. This applies to [Department of the Army] Civilians, Soldiers and their Families, local populations, victims of natural disasters, and enemy combatants. Empathy enhances cultural understanding and enables an Army leader to better interact with others.[37]

Here, there is an attempt to distinguish empathy from sympathy, though it seems undermined by the other statement that describes empathy as identifying with "another person's feelings and emotions." Identification is offered as something that contributes to understanding, but taken as a whole, this explanation of empathy appears subject to the concerns of agreement and care highlighted above.

It is striking that this doctrinal reference acknowledges empathy's help in understanding enemies. This point parallels Waldman's above that there is a way of empathetically understanding an enemy in addition to noncombatants and allies (helpfully illustrated by Hugh Thompson interrupting the My Lai Massacre). I think this controversial suggestion is correct and spend the next two chapters trying to explain why.

Military theory, international relations theory, and Army doctrine all illustrate the variety of conceptions about empathy, and they reflect the variety one finds in empathy scholarship. This variety is problematic for soldiers trying to take seriously the doctrinal emphasis on empathy. In particular, it is unclear how a soldier should "identify with," "care about," or "relate to" noncombatants and, especially, enemies. Prompted by these references to identification, caring, and relation, even the call to merely understand others can be misconstrued to entail acceptance instead of just comprehension. I have in mind the phrase "Well, that's understandable" that one might utter after listening to a friend's confusion or remorse over some minor wrongdoing she committed. The connotation is that one accepts or finds reasonable the friend's thoughts and feelings that led to the behavior, which is one step beyond simply comprehending the thoughts and feelings.

Empathy may amplify the moral sensitivity of soldiers by underscoring the humanity of enemies and various noncombatants in the war environment. Alternatively, a more selective empathy may promote soldiers' devotion to their in-group at the illegitimate expense of outsiders, whether combatants or noncombatants. In either case, empathy's contribution to soldiers' behavior seems dubious. Thus, I want to offer a fuller examination of empathy, its nature, and its relation to war, partly to defend its appearance in US Army doctrine.

The Risk of Moral Injury

As a final introductory effort, I want to present the notion of moral injury among soldiers as a serious concern in arguing that they should be empathetic. Moral injury refers to pain rooted in one's psyche that "attaches to an individual's sense of agency."[38] It is a wound to a person's self-esteem, self-worth, or self-trust; it undermines a person's confidence in her own goodness. It can produce symptoms like those of post-traumatic stress disorder (PTSD), including persistent emotional distress, emotional numbing, depression, nightmares, nervousness, and an inability to conduct normal daily life. However, moral injury also involves reactive attitudes like extreme anger and resentment (often self-oriented), as well as moral emotions like grief, guilt, and remorse.[39] PTSD stems from intense fear commonly associated with a life-threatening event, but moral injury stems from guilt over some action taken, not taken, or even something merely witnessed. It is a perceived moral failing. Morally injured veterans speak of the futility of their efforts to accomplish the mission, the grief of killing another human being (especially noncombatants), the remorse of abandoning wounded civilians, or the betrayal by a superior who issued a flawed order. Fear is noticeably absent from the accounts of the morally injured.[40]

What is noticeably present is a theme of tragedy and subsequent guilt. I offer five examples of moral injury to illustrate this "bruise on the soul."[41] I will then use these examples to build a rudimentary taxonomy of moral injury.

Shay's CIB Recipient

Psychiatrist Jonathan Shay shares the firsthand account of a soldier in Vietnam:

> Now, there was a LURP [Long Range Reconnaissance Patrol] team from the First Brigade off of Highway One, that looked over the South China Sea. There was a bay there .... Now, they saw boats come in. And they suspected, now, uh – the word came down [that] they were unloading weapons off them. Three boats.
>
> At that time we moved. It was about ten o'clock at night. We moved down, across Highway One along the beach line, and it took us [until] about three or four o'clock in the morning to get on line while these people are unloading their boats. And we opened up on them – aaah.
>
> And the fucking firepower was unreal, the firepower that we put into them boats. It was just a constant, constant firepower. It seemed like no one ever ran out of ammo.
>
> Daylight came [long pause], and we found out we killed a lot of fishermen and kids.
>
> What got us thoroughly fucking confused is, at that time you turn to the team and you say to the team, "Don't worry about it. Everything's fucking fine." Because that's what you're getting from upstairs.
>
> The fucking colonel says, "Don't worry about it. We'll take care of it." Y'know, uh, "We got body count!" "We have body count!" So it starts working on your head. So you know in your heart it's wrong, but at the time, here's your superiors telling you that it was okay. So, I mean, that's okay then, right? This is part of war. Y'know? Gung-HO! Y'know? AirBORNE! AirBORNE! Let's go!
>
> So we packed up and we moved out.

They wanted to give us a fucking Unit Citation – them fucking maggots. A lot of medals came down from it. The lieutenants got their medals, and I know the colonel got his fucking medal. And they would have award ceremonies, y'know, I'd be standing like a fucking jerk and they'd be handing out fucking medals for killing civilians.[42]

Shay adds: "This veteran received his Combat Infantry Badge for participating in this action. The CIB was one of the most prized US Army awards, supposed to be awarded for actual engagement in ground combat."[43]

Romeo Dallaire

In 1993, the United Nations sent a small, multinational military force into Rwanda to monitor a peace agreement established between the warring Hutu and Tutsi ethnic groups. This force was commanded by Canadian Lieutenant General Romeo Dallaire. As tensions rose and suspicions grew, Dallaire lobbied his Canadian and UN leadership for more soldiers, more resources, and more leeway to keep the peace that he was charged to protect.[44] His requests were repeatedly denied over the next year. His diplomatic attempts to stave off the rising battle cries among Hutu and Tutsi extremists fell short, and his military operations to confiscate weapons and disrupt extremist plots were forbidden by his risk-averse and indifferent political supervisors. The Rwandan president was assassinated in April 1994, which sparked extremist Hutus to massacre at least 800,000 Tutsis and moderate Hutus over the next three months. Dallaire and his contingent of armed but administratively restrained soldiers stood "literally in the middle of the slaughter for weeks on end."[45] They did not, however, stand still. Through their limited means, they protected over 30,000 individuals, even as further requests for reinforcement were consistently and abruptly turned down.[46]

Dallaire remains anguished by "how ineffective and irresponsible we were when we promised the Rwandans that we would establish an atmosphere of security that would allow them to achieve a lasting peace." Following the catastrophe, he writes:

I have yearned to return to Rwanda and disappear into the blue-green hills with my ghosts. But as I slowly begin to piece my life back together, I know the time has come for me to make a more difficult pilgrimage: to travel back through all those terrible memories and retrieve my soul.

[In the years following the genocide,] I plunged into a disastrous mental health spiral that led me to suicide attempts, a medical release from the Armed Forces, the diagnosis of post-traumatic stress disorder, and dozens upon dozens of therapy sessions and extensive medication, which still have a place in my daily life.

It took me seven years to finally have the desire, the will-power and the stamina to begin to describe in detail the events of that year in Rwanda… [and] how the international community, through an inept UN mandate and what can only be described as indifference, self-interest and racism, aided and abetted these crimes against humanity – how we all helped create the mess that has murdered and displaced millions and destabilized the whole central African region.[47]

Shay's Seasoned Soldier

I return to Shay for the story of a Vietnam veteran who is tormented by the following memory (I will refer to him as the "seasoned soldier"):

[The seasoned soldier entered] a village from the south while other, inexperienced soldiers were entering it from the east. A Vietnamese baby was sitting in the crossroads at the center of the village. [The seasoned soldier] could see remote trigger wires running to the spot under the baby and began to shout and wave his arms at the other soldiers not to go near the baby. The other soldiers could not hear and simply waved back. Seeing no alternative, [the seasoned soldier] fired a burst from his M-60 into the baby, setting off a large explosion.[48]

Nik Rudolph

Journalist David Wood shares Nik Rudolph's experience while in Afghanistan:

Broad shouldered and lean at six foot two, Nikki Rudolph, an affable sandy-haired Californian, was twenty-two years old when he was sent as a marine infantryman to Afghanistan, where he shot and killed a young boy. This was not uncommon in the murderous confusion of our recent wars, where farmers and mothers and young kids might seize a weapon and shape-shift in a moment into a combatant and back again to an innocent civilian, and young Americans peering into the murk would have a moment to decide: kill or not. This time, an exhausting firefight with Taliban insurgents had dragged on for hours across the superheated desert wastes and tree-lined irrigation canals of Helmand Province. Late that afternoon, Nik saw from the corner of his eye someone darting around the corner of an adobe wall, spraying bullets from an assault rifle held against his small hips. Nik swiveled his M4 carbine, tightened his finger on the trigger, and saw that it was a boy of maybe twelve or thirteen. Then he fired.[49]

John Lee

Wood also recounts the story of World War II veteran John Lee:

In the waning days of World War II, Private First Class John Lee and other American GIs assembled about sixty German soldiers, lined them up against a brick wall, and, as the Germans stood with their hands raised in surrender, shot them down in fusillades of fire.

These were no ordinary Wehrmacht troops; they were fanatical Nazi SS soldiers. The Americans had just broken into the notorious death camp at Dachau, where the SS served as guards... The German SS troopers were grinning and taunting the Americans. It seemed unlikely, in those chaotic last days of the war, that the SS men would ever be brought to real justice for the crimes they had committed .... [Lee] acknowledged that killing the German prisoners had been wrong. He readily acknowledged the guilt and regret of moral injury and the pain of having held his secret for so long ....

He described how he and his unit, India Company of the 3rd Battalion, 157th Infantry Regiment, had fought almost continuously for more than a year, landing at Anzio in Italy and fighting up through France and on into Germany. Ordered to secure what they were told was a local prison, they scaled masonry walls to find thirty-six boxcars of rotting corpses, inmates who'd been starved. It was overcast and chilly, Lee remembered, as he and the others crept forward beneath tall pines, finding more stacks of bodies and atrocities of which some soldiers could not speak even decades later. By the time they began rounding up the prison guards, as the thirty-two thousand gaunt inmates still living cheered and jeered from behind fences, the men of India Company were "boiling mad, half out of our minds," one soldier said later. Lee told me, "I looked at the bodies as we went past – their open eyes seemed to say, *What took you so long?*" As the men walked warily deeper into the camp, somebody muttered, "No prisoners!" Eventually, they rounded up the Germans. As Lee remembered it, there was "a deathly silence. We lined up the SS guards. One of the guys cocked the machine gun. The Germans started moving and somebody shouted 'Fire!'"[50]

As a basic taxonomy, I want to propose three possible routes to moral injury: tragic betrayal, tragic right-doing, and tragic self-betrayal. I will clarify these categories by connecting them with the five examples above and the literature on moral injury. I will then conclude with an examination of the guilt and grief inherent to the moral injury of all three routes.

Tragic Betrayal

Shay's recipient of the Combat Infantry Badge (CIB) and Romeo Dallaire are examples of tragic betrayal. Shay focuses his research on this route, defining moral injury as the betrayal of moral norms in a "high-stakes" situation by those in authority.[51] Shay highlights the reverberating effects of "leadership malpractice" on subordinates, including intense rage, loss of trust, and thwarted grief. These effects result in the "undoing of character" and create "the desire to do things that [the soldier] himself regarded as bad."[52] It is important to separate the moral injury due to the initial betrayal from subsequent wrongdoing that the soldier may commit of his own accord. Guilt remains inappropriate for the soldier in this initial betrayal; it ostensibly gains purchase in subsequent wrongdoing. While it is important to consider the soldier's experience in its totality, it is also important to separate the initial moral injury of these soldiers from the moral transgressions that they may commit. For one thing, the moral injury is an important consideration in understanding the soldier's subsequent behavior (which is precisely Shay's motivation). For another, the moral injury requires a specific remedy that may differ from any rectification of the subsequent behavior.

In the case of the CIB recipient, the soldier did not know that the information about the individuals on the boats was in error. If the person providing the information, or a member of the chain of command receiving the information, knew the error or knowingly portrayed the peaceful boat activity as a legitimate target, then the culpability belongs to them, not to the soldier, even though the soldier participated in the wrong action. Alternatively, culpability may not be so easily attributable, since the information may sincerely have been in error. Regardless of how the attack on the boats came about, the betrayal of moral norms was, at the least, in the leaders' dishonest and callous attempts to overlook the killing of civilians, and in fact reward the soldier for his participation.

Romeo Dallaire's story also involves dishonesty and callousness on the part of superiors. Furthermore, it demonstrates that the betrayal inherent to this type of moral injury can occur through the superiors' exercise of too much restraint and not merely too little (as the excesses of war more commonly show). Either extreme is a violation of moral norms governing the use of lethal force. Unlike the CIB recipient's case, it is far easier to identify those guilty for the wrongdoing that involved Dallaire. His account, which is corroborated by others,[53] incriminates member nations of the UN Security Council, other leaders within the international community, and key figures within Rwanda. Despite this clarity, Dallaire felt incapacitating guilt himself.

The betrayal on the part of a superior (or, conceivably, military peers or noncombatants) can be spurred by the dehumanization so ordinary to modern war.[54] This factor is unclear in the case of Shay's CIB recipient; the leaders' appeal to body count and the conferral of commendation awards could have been motivated by a stubborn unwillingness to admit the wrong of killing civilians, or, perhaps, an overpowering concern to protect the soldiers from guilt and maintain their motivation. However, even this stubbornness or this guarding of the soldier's morale would be easier if the Vietnamese were dehumanized in the minds of the superiors.

Dehumanization is clearer in Dallaire's case. When he received an envoy of bureaucrats in the first weeks of the genocide, they concluded, "We will recommend to our government not to intervene as the risks are high and all that is here are [merely] humans."[55]

In another instance, Dallaire explains:

> I had one person come into my headquarters during the genocide asking [for] statistics on how many people were killed last week and how many yesterday and how many do you expect to be killed today and how many weeks of this killing you think is going to go on. And my staff officers brought him to me and I said, "Why

these statistics?" He said, "Oh, you know my country is assessing whether it will come in and the government believes that the people [of my country], the public opinion, could handle for every soldier killed or injured an equivalent of 85,000 dead Rwandans."[56]

Moments of tragic betrayal are moments of moral transgressions. The culpability, though, lies with the ones who betrayed the soldier. The soldier is *morally* innocent even if not *materially* innocent.[57] This fact is small consolation to the morally injured soldier, who recognizes the wrongness of the action, is incensed by it and his own contribution to it, and suffers under the emphasis within military culture on doing one's duty and offering no excuses when failing to do so. This emphasis is heightened for commanders like Dallaire, since the common mantra is that a military commander is responsible for all that his unit does and fails to do. International humanitarian law has formalized this burden of command responsibility through precedents such as the Nuremberg trials after World War II.[58] Both military culture and established law combine to make some soldiers caught up in tragic betrayal feel tremendously guilty and doubt their very identity as agents oriented toward the good.

Tragic Right-Doing

Shay's seasoned soldier and Nik Rudolph are examples of tragic right-doing. I hesitate to use the prefix "right" in this way, given the grievous choices facing these two veterans, but it seems necessary to convey the lack of moral wrongdoing. In cases of tragic right-doing, soldiers suffer despite the justified nature of the act, caught in "the fatal conflict of two valid claims."[59] Shay's seasoned soldier was stuck between the safety of his comrades and the safety of the Vietnamese baby. Furthermore, he was stuck with the urgency of the moment, seeing no way to accommodate even some degree of safety for all. One might appraise his choice as morally wrong since he favored the well-being of his fellow soldiers over that of a clearly innocent noncombatant. It is the nature of soldiering, one might say, for soldiers to take on the risk that would otherwise fall to civilians, especially vulnerable children. Others might defend the seasoned soldier by emphasizing his contextual influences, especially a natural loyalty to his comrades, or by noting that he was not the one to expose the child to this danger – the responsibility falls to the enemies who placed the baby on top of the explosive device. In addition, the soldier's choice protected two lives instead of allowing all three lives to be lost.

For my purposes, the resolution of this debate does not matter. If the seasoned soldier committed a moral transgression, then his story becomes a case of tragic self-betrayal (see below) instead of tragic right-doing. Moral or legal censure seems inappropriate for this soldier, whether his act is considered wrong or right. The precariousness of the moral status is itself an important factor in moral injury, since it increases the burden on the soldier who struggles to make sense of the act.

Rudolph's case is somewhat less contentious because the child he killed was an active combatant. Yet the precariousness still haunts Rudolph. It is worth returning to Wood's account:

> According to the military's exacting legal principles and rules, it was a justifiable kill, even laudable, an action taken against an enemy combatant in defense of Nik himself and his fellow marines. But now Nik is back home in civilian life, where killing a child violates the bedrock moral ideals we all hold.[60]

These cases give a particularly gruesome color to the moral dilemmas of war.[61] They highlight the tragedy of facing decisions between morally problematic options, famously illustrated by Philippa Foot's "trolley problem," in which a trolley driver is faced with the choice of allowing the trolley to continue on its current track and run over five individuals or switching the trolley onto a new track to run over only a single individual.[62] The thought experiment has generated decades of scrutiny and debate, fostering rich discussions about doing vs. allowing harm, intending vs. foreseeing the good and bad effects of one's action, and the choice between greater and lesser evils.[63] My focus is not on the dilemmas themselves, nor on how soldiers ought to make them, nor on how the rest of us ought to judge the decisions made. Instead, my focus is on a dangerous repercussion of those decisions: moral injury. Soldiers do not always anticipate the grief and loss inherent to the decisions confronting them. They may see one choice as morally unproblematic. The reality, though, is that even a legitimate act of lethal force is only *legally* unproblematic. The death of adversaries, or of noncombatants accidentally killed, is the death of human beings. It is still a moral loss, regardless of its justification.

Soldiers involved in tragic right-doing feel this loss after the fact even if they are blind to it prior. In the case of Shay's seasoned soldier, he seems to have been aware of the moral loss in each of his options right away. Rudolph's tragic choice crept up on him "only later, well after he'd pulled the trigger, [when] the implications of what he'd done began to weigh on him."[64] This retrospective regret can surprise soldiers trained and cultured to see their soldierly duties as without moral blemish, as straightforwardly heroic. In one scholar's words:

> The morally injured subject...does not know that they will view their actions after the fact as wrong and harmful. There is a shock, even a break, to moral injury where the way one had understood the moral ecology of the world prior to their injurious experience is found retrospectively to be incorrect. This can create a moral cognitive dissonance raising doubt concerning one's continuing ability to strive to be good or whether goodness can occur in the world at all.[65]

The soldier's shock is an indication of the "moral residue" that remains after facing dilemmatic choices.[66] The residue is not erroneous – it is appropriate for an agent facing a "trolley problem" choice to feel grief or guilt, no matter his decision. In this regard, morally injured soldiers demonstrate a respectable attunement to the moral dimensions of their decisions. It is inappropriate for an agent to remain indifferent to the moral loss inherent to his choice.

What is also inappropriate is the attempt to make the soldier's decision easier by disguising the moral loss involved. One veteran expressed this concern by complaining "something is wrong with what's right."[67] I take his complaint to be "something is [morally] wrong with what [is portrayed by military training, military culture, and the larger social culture to be morally] right." In this regard, tragic right-doing also involves a kind of betrayal, even if less directly than tragic betrayal above. The betrayal is by those individuals or groups who hide the tragic nature of war, who present the soldier's moral decisions as between a positively good option and an evil option, instead of an option between two evils (to use premodern terminology). The lesser evil is deceptively (perhaps also shallowly, blandly, or crassly) cast in an overly positive light. Wood warns that in our culture "we have constructed an image of war in which its vileness is airbrushed away."[68] There is a subtle betrayal in blinding soldiers to the moral residue entailed by their duties and the corresponding gravity of their choices.

The difficulty, however, is that the betrayer is more anonymous and not a single individual. The deception is expressed mutedly in military doctrine and training, bureaucratic policy, political propaganda, and popular culture. This anonymity and multiplicity of the betrayer can make the moral injury of tragic right-doing more intractable because the soldier cannot point to the specific deceiver, only to the deception itself. The fact of the deception and yet the vagueness of its source can prompt the soldier to attribute the moral insensitivity to himself, thus driving the self-doubt about "one's continuing ability to strive to be good" noted above. This effect is particularly ironic since the soldier's sensitivity is what makes him react to the moral residue of tragic right-doing in the first place.

I want to briefly gesture at three sources of overly positive light that blinds soldiers to the morally problematic choices they face (as well as blinding the societies they represent): dehumanization, romantic notions of war, and militarism. The dehumanization of enemies or noncombatants, as noted already, is widespread in modern war, partly due to a pragmatic conviction that "dehumanizing removes psychological barriers from the killing that combat requires, and it provides the soldier a bulwark against psychological damage."[69] Moral injury illustrates that removing such barriers can actually prompt psychological damage. I will save a full consideration of dehumanization and its shortcomings for Chapter 3. For now, I simply point to its potential role in making soldiers susceptible to the shock of moral dilemmas. (Admittedly, the moral injury through tragic right-doing does not have to involve dehumanization. For instance, it is not necessarily involved in the cases of Shay's seasoned soldier or Nik Rudolph.)

Second, war can easily take on a hue of heroism, of nobility, and of being something better than it really is, for a variety of complicated reasons and histories. This romanticized notion takes root easier among those who join the military out of a strong sense of service. Furthermore, military training often promotes a romantic sense of war to instill a fervent devotion in recruits. Society's expressions of respect for soldiers can also reinforce an idealized view of war. Regarding moral injury, an overly romantic view of war makes it easier to neglect its moral costs.

Finally, a veiled militarism can twist the soldier's moment of tragic right-doing into a moment where, allegedly, no tragic choice exists. As A.J. Coates observes, militarism is a...

> cultural bias in favour of war... [war is] a positive good (and not a lesser evil), something of intrinsic and unique value, worthy of being willed not as a regrettable means to some higher, external and pacific goal, but as an end in itself.[70]

Such an attitude is most blatant in fascist ideology, but, as Coates points out, there are nonfascist forms of militarism, in which religious, ideological, or paternalistic devotion can propel a dangerously enthusiastic embrace of war. This predisposition toward war's necessity and its benefits can obscure its moral ambiguity.

In cases of tragic right-doing, the burden of war's moral dilemmas can haunt soldiers to the point of incapacitation, especially if the grief of those dilemmas comes as a shock. The rightness of their decision may be eclipsed by the unexpected moral residue that sticks with them, prompting a persistent doubt of their own judgment. This doubt can fester into a larger uncertainty regarding their own agency and whether they are capable of pursuing goodness at all.

Tragic Self-betrayal

While Shay emphasizes the moral injury due to betrayal by superiors, others have focused on a route of tragic self-betrayal.[71] The betrayer is oneself instead of another, involving a moral transgression that a soldier commits of his own accord, despite a general disposition of good character. This route to moral injury tracks the former route of tragic right-doing very closely in terms of a stark moral dilemma, the precariousness of an action's true moral status, the urgency of a decision, and the enduring moral residue after the incident. The difference is simply in the outcome of the conflict between competing moral requirements. Due to various factors, the soldier transgresses moral norms and feels the weight of his conscience.

The transgression is genuine, but tragic self-betrayal differs from a war crime. The transgression carries significant moral warrant that combines with various extenuating circumstances, as illustrated by John Lee's story. Lee and his unit were overwhelmed by the atrocities against the prisoners, the maddening attitude of the SS soldiers, and the exhaustion of nearly a year of fighting. This self-inflicted moral injury underscores the fragility of good character in the face of extreme demands. Contrary to the persistent myth that "good character cannot change... [and that no] bad experience can break it," individual character is vulnerable to the buffeting effects of this world, particularly in war.[72] Sometimes good soldiers get agonizingly tough moral decisions wrong. These cases raise questions concerning the limits of morality's demandingness in nonideal conditions.[73] The specific tragedy of this kind of moral injury, however, is when the soldier offers himself no relief by recognizing those limits. In light of the transgression, he tries to balance the scales of justice through self-punishment.

Sometimes, the soldier might have some appreciation for his own fallibility and recognize the weight of external influences. As Wood observes:

> The US military has spent years and fortunes perfecting the most realistic and thorough combat training in the world. But in preparing young Americans for war, it has failed in one glaring aspect. Those we send to war are never trained to anticipate the moral quandaries of killing that they will face; they are given no opportunity or encouragement to think about or to discuss what makes some killings moral and others a sin or even illegal.[74]

In this vein, tragic self-betrayal resembles tragic betrayal, in that the soldier may come to view himself as tricked by a subtle cultural deception or insensitivity. Like tragic right-doing, though, the betrayal is indirect, since the betrayer is more anonymous and multiplicitous, grounded in social norms and expectations. Unlike tragic right-doing, the soldier has genuinely committed a moral transgression, making guilt appropriate, but also making it easier for him to slip into a form of self-loathing that leaves no room for restoration and self-forgiveness.

The Guilt of Moral Injury

By underscoring the tragedy of these three routes to moral injury, I mean to emphasize that "moral injury" is not a glib term for the awakening conscience of a war criminal. As Wood observes, "Moral injury does not imply that an atrocity or a war crime has been committed, simply that an individual's ethos has been violated."[75] Morally injured veterans strive to abide by the established rules of engagement, exhibit respectable moral reasoning and commitment, and perform well under the pressure of excruciating circumstances. War criminals fall short in one or more of these areas. A war criminal might suffer something akin to moral injury. Yet this debilitating guilt would be fitting instead of misplaced. The guilt felt by the morally injured soldier is puzzling in the cases of tragic betrayal and tragic right-doing, since the soldier is not actually culpable for some wrong done. In moments of tragic self-betrayal, the guilt is not a puzzle, but the reaction to that guilt can be out of proportion to the circumstances.

To make sense of this feeling of culpability yet no objective guilt, it is important to consider Eleonore Stump's insight that in the consequences of our actions "harm and injustice can come apart."[76] While harm and injustice typically go together, in some circumstances there can be harm done with no injustice. She illustrates:

> Suppose, for example, Paula and her young child have been assigned separate seats on a long flight but that they could sit together if Jerome would trade seats with one of them, and suppose also that he can do so at no cost of any kind to himself, not even the inconvenience of moving his possessions. (Imagine, for the sake of the thought experiment, that Jerome has not yet stowed them around his own assigned seat). It is clear that Paula has no right to Jerome's seat, and so Jerome does not do her an injustice if he refuses to trade seats with her. But he has done her some harm, since he has made it more difficult for her to care for the needs of her child.[77]

Moral injury is another instance when harm and injustice can come apart. In cases of tragic betrayal, there has been both harm and injustice, but the injustice falls to the superiors who betrayed moral norms. In cases of tragic right-doing, a soldier is struggling with the harm of her actions, even though there is no injustice. In these two routes to moral injury, the soldiers are right to grieve the harm they did, though they are not responsible for an injustice; therefore, genuine guilt does not apply. Grief is the better description. In cases of tragic self-betrayal, both guilt and grief are appropriate, but not to the point of debilitating the soldier's agency.

The Grief of Moral Injury

Soldiers struggle with the grief that is inherent to war, no matter the justification of the specific wars in which they find themselves, and no matter the justification for the tactical actions they participate in. (If the war's justification is in doubt, or the tactics involved, then this grief may be greater.) As Mark Wilson argues, this grief ought to be considered an appropriate response to war and "an important capacity for a well-formed character."[78] Grief, in this regard, is a virtue, reflecting the soldiers' recognition of what is good, as well as a corresponding recognition that war is always regrettable.[79]

Soldiers who grieve war and their participation in it are often not prepared to handle this virtuous response or even see it as such.[80] If unable to process the grief that arises, to include misinterpreting it as an indication of guilt, soldiers will have a tendency to slip from grief to either "unchecked self-loathing" or "unthinking apathy."[81] One way of describing the slip toward unchecked self-loathing is to say that the soldier is questioning his true self, beginning to identify himself with bad instead of good desires and capacities. As this identification drifts toward unchecked self-loathing, feelings of grief become overwhelming and result in moral injury. (With tragic self-betrayal, genuine guilt adds to the grief and self-condemnation.) Caught in feeling the grief as guilt, the unchecked self-loathing can be an attempt at self-punishment.

One may want to describe the slip in the other direction toward unthinking apathy as a kind of moral injury, as well. It is a deadening of one's moral sense and is reminiscent of some recent veterans' conclusion that war simply demands that soldiers "push past [ostensibly] immoral behavior" until "it becomes easier."[82] However, for most soldiers, even if they approach unthinking apathy, it is never for very long. As cases of moral injury attest, their consciences catch up with them in what Wilson calls "reflective suffering" and they are left trying to make sense of the grief and feelings of guilt that can propel them toward unchecked self-loathing.[83]

Conclusion

While I began this introduction by noting empathy's uneasy position in American military culture, I want to end it by noting the empathy exercised by many soldiers in practice, even if unconsciously or uncertainly. Consider the story of a soldier of mine from a deployment to Iraq in 2003.

Our unit received information that an individual who lived in our assigned area had been an army colonel in Saddam Hussein's regime. After the invasion of Iraq, this colonel had begun planning and funding the insurgent efforts around his hometown. I joined the other commanders and staff in planning a raid on the colonel's home. My soldiers would enter his house in the early morning, subdue everyone present, arrest the colonel, and search the house. Once security was set around the neighborhood, our higher command initiated the operation. My soldiers kicked in the front door and scanned every corner.

"Stop!" one soldier yelled in Arabic. A crouched man was rushing into the entry room. He was bent over, his hands were hidden, he was lunging forward...and then two of the four soldiers shot him and he fell to the floor. Those were the only shots fired. Thirty seconds later, the house was secure and the team began rendering first aid to the fallen man. He died in front of them – and in front of his wife and young daughter, who had been found in the home and brought to the entry room. The dead man was the Iraqi colonel.

That man's death remained with the soldiers who shot him. One of the soldiers, in particular, wrestled with the death that he caused. The chain of command agreed that the team's actions were justified, but that did not lessen the weight my soldier felt. The man he killed was not carrying anything in his hands. My soldier struggled to understand why the man lunged toward him. Was the colonel attempting to protect his family? Was he trying to tackle the lead soldier coming through the door? Was he entering the room to investigate the loud noise? Did he simply trip as he entered to room? My soldier reminded me that he himself had a wife and a young daughter, and he could not help but wonder what would happen to this colonel's family.

This soldier's struggle is an example of the empathy that commonly occurs in war, even if it goes largely unrecognized in our theorizing about war. It is a natural response to war's regrettable duties, yet military training is too often focused on repressing these reactions to ensure soldiers persist in their duties – better a thoughtless soldier instead of one too thoughtful. I want to resist this conclusion; either extreme is just as detrimental to good soldiering. While some will maintain that I should have steered my soldier away from his empathetic response to the colonel's death, I want to show the benefit of that response, both for the soldier's own good and for the good of the war effort. I grant that such a response taken to an extreme can be detrimental. I am glad to report that this soldier was able to continue participating in our unit's patrols and combat actions, but I find it just as important to consider *why* he was able to continue. It was not that he simply became indifferent to the gravity of his duties; he allowed that gravity to shape his conduct. As a result, I could trust him to a greater extent than I could before.

My goal, then, is to fix the gap in military theory that fails to account for the value of empathy. I aim to explain how empathy is compatible with military duties and improves the judgment and performance of military personnel. Such theoretical work can foster a more conscious and uninhibited embrace of empathy by soldiers and by the citizens they represent.

As my former soldier came to realize, war is tragic. This aspect is largely overshadowed by a tendency to dehumanize enemies, to idealize war's possibilities, and to neglect a full consideration of war's moral dimensions in military training and in American society at large. Given this confusion, moral injury is a virtually guaranteed cost of any war. Still, not every veteran carries debilitating guilt, even if they feel the pain of the harms that war inflicts on others. These veterans are able to cope with the grief of war. Do they lose this ability by pursuing an empathetic understanding of others, especially enemies and noncombatants? In other words, does empathy upset the balance that allowed my former soldier to persist in his duties? A sufficient answer must start with a deeper consideration of empathy.

Works Cited

Aquinas, Thomas (1485). *Summa theologiae*. Trans. Fathers of the English Dominican Province. Second and Revised Edition, 1920. Online Edition Copyright © 2008 by Kevin Knight. <http://www.newadvent.org/summa/>.

Biggar, Nigel (2013). *In Defence of War*. Oxford: Oxford University Press.

Brough, Michael (2007). "Dehumanization of the Enemy and the Moral Equality of Soldiers." *Rethinking the Just War Tradition*. Eds. Michael Brough, John Lango, Harry van der Linden. Albany: State University of New York Press, 149–167.

Coates, A.J. (2016). *The Ethics of War*. 2nd ed. Manchester: Manchester University Press.

Dahl, Hanne Marlene (2000). "A Perceptive or Reflective State?" *European Journal of Women's Studies,* Vol. 7, No. 4, 475–494.

Dallaire, Romeo (2004). *Shake Hands with the Devil: The Failure of Humanity in Rwanda.* New York: Carrol & Graff Publishers.

Dallaire, Romeo (2002). "A Good Man in Hell: General Roméo Dallaire and the Rwanda Genocide," Interview with Ted Koppel, US Holocaust Memorial Museum (12 June 2002). <https://www.ushmm.org/confront-genocide/speakers-and-events/all-speakers-and-events/a-good-man-in-hell-general-romeo-dallaire-and-the-rwanda-genocide>.

Dokoupil, Tony (2012). "Moral Injury." *Newsweek* (10 December 2012).

Dubik, James (2016). *Just War Reconsidered – Strategy, Ethics, and Theory.* Lexington: University Press of Kentucky.

Foot, Philippa (1978). *Virtues and Vices and Other Essays.* Berkeley: University of California Press.

French, Shannon (2017). *The Code of the Warrior: Exploring Warrior Values Past and Present.* 2nd ed. Lanham, MD: Rowman and Littlefield.

Goldie, Peter (2002). *The Emotions: A Philosophical Exploration.* New York: Oxford University Press.

Henneberger, Melinda (2014). "Canada's Romeo Dallaire Is Honored For His Attempts to Halt Rwandan Genocide in 1994." *The Washington Post* (1 May 2014). <https://www.washingtonpost.com/politics/canadas-romeo-dallaire-is-honored-for-his-attempts-to-halt-rwandan-genocide-in-1994/2014/05/01/fe4f7d8a-d13e-11e3-9e25-188ebe1fa93b_story.html?noredirect=on&utm_term= .3a8faf6f6236>.

Kahl, Colin (2007). "COIN of the Realm: Is There a Future for Counterinsurgency?" *Foreign Affairs* (November/December 2007). <https://www.foreignaffairs.com/reviews/review-essay/2007-11-01/coin-realm>.

Litz, Brett T., Nathan Stein, Eileen Delaney, Leslie Lebowitz, William P. Nash, Caroline Silva, and Shira Maguen (2009). "Moral Injury and Moral Repair in War Veterans: A Preliminary Model and Intervention Strategy." *Clinical Psychology Review*, Vol. 29, 695–706.

McConnell, Terrance (2014). "Moral Dilemmas." *Stanford Encyclopedia of Philosophy*. Ed. Edward Zalta (Fall 2014). <https://plato.stanford.edu/archives/fall2014/entries/moral-dilemmas/>.

McGreal, Chris (1999). "Investigators Condemn UN Chief for 'Deplorable' Inaction in Rwanda." *The Guardian* (16 December 1999). <https://www.theguardian.com/world/1999/dec/17/ chrismcgreall>.

McMahan, Jeff (1996). "Realism, Morality, and War." *The Ethics of War and Peace*. Ed. Terry Nardin. Princeton, NJ: Princeton University Press, 78–92.

Nussbaum, Martha (1986). *The Fragility of Goodness: Luck and Ethics in Greek Tragedy and Philosophy*. New York: Cambridge University Press.

Orend, Brian (2013). *The Morality of War*. 2nd ed. Toronto: Broadview Press.

Power, Samantha (2001). "Bystanders to Genocide." *The Atlantic* (September 2001). <https://www.theatlantic.com/magazine/archive/2001/09/bystanders-to-genocide/304571/>.

Scales, Robert (2006). "Clausewitz and World War IV." *Armed Forces Journal* (July 2006). <http://www.armedforcesjournal.com/2006/07/1866019>.

Shay, Jonathan (2014). "Moral Injury." *Psychoanalytic Psychology*, Vol. 31, no. 2, 182–191.

Shay, Jonathan (1994). *Achilles in Vietnam: Combat Trauma and the Undoing of Character*. New York: Simon and Schuster.

Sjoberg, Laura (2013). *Gendering Global Conflict: Toward a Feminist Theory of War*. New York: Columbia University Press.

Stump, Eleonore (2018). *Atonement*. New York: Oxford University Press.

Sylvester, Christine (1994). *Feminist Theory and International Relations in a Postmodern Era*. Cambridge: Cambridge University Press.

US Army Field Manual 3-24, *Counterinsurgency*. Fort Leavenworth: Combined Arms Doctrine Directorate, 2006.

US Army Field Manual 3-24, *Insurgencies and Countering Insurgencies*. Fort Leavenworth: Combined Arms Doctrine Directorate, 2014.

US Army Field Manual 3-07.1, *Security Force Assistance*. Fort Leavenworth: Combined Arms Doctrine Directorate, 2009.

US Army Doctrinal Publication 6-22, *Army Leadership and the Profession*. Fort Leavenworth: Combined Arms Doctrine Directorate, 2019.

US Army Doctrinal Reference Publication 2-0, *Intelligence*. Fort Leavenworth: Combined Arms Doctrine Directorate, 2012.

US Army Doctrinal Reference Publication 5-0, *The Operations Process*. Fort Leavenworth: Combined Arms Doctrine Directorate, 2012.

US Army Field Manual 3-13, *Inform and Influence Activities*. Fort Leavenworth: Combined Arms Doctrine Directorate, 2013.

US Army Field Manual 6–22, *Leader Development*. Fort Leavenworth: Combined Arms Doctrine Directorate, 2015.

US Army Training and Doctrine Command (2017). "Multi-Domain Battle: Combined Arms for the 21st Century," Information Paper, 4. Fort Eustis: Training and Doctrine Command. <http://www.tradoc.army.mil/multido-mainbattle/docs/ MDB_WhitePaper.pdf>.

van Ackeren, Marcel, and Michael Kuhler, eds. (2016). *The Limits of Moral Obligation: Moral Demandingness and Ought Implies Can.* New York: Routledge.

Verkamp, Bernard (1993). *The Moral Treatment of Returning Warriors in Early Medieval and Modern Times.* Scranton: University of Scranton Press.

Vetlesen, Arne Johan (1994). *Perception, Empathy, and Judgment.* University Park, PA: Pennsylvania State University Press.

Waldman, Matt (2014). "Strategic Empathy: The Afghanistan Intervention Shows Why the US Must Empathize With Its Enemies." New America Foundation (April 2014). <https://static.newamerica.org/attach-ments/4350-strategic-empathy-2/Waldman%20Strategic%20Empathy_2.3caa1c3d706143f1a8cae6a7d2ce70c7.pdf.>

Walzer, Michael (2015 [1977]). *Just and Unjust Wars: A Moral Argument with Historical Illustrations.* 5th ed. New York: Basic Books.

Wiinikka-Lydon, Joseph (2018). "Dirty Hands and Moral Injury." *Philosophy,* Vol. 93, no. 3 (March 2018), 1–20.

Wilkinson, Judith (1987). "Moral Distress in Nursing Practice: Experience and Effect." *Nursing Forum,* Vol. 23, no. 1 (April 1987), 16–29.

Williams, Bernard (2006). *Ethics and the Limits of Philosophy.* New York: Routledge.

Williams, Bernard (1965). "Ethical Consistency." *Proceedings of the Aristotelian Society* (1965 Supplement). Vol. 39, 103–124.

Williamson, Jamie (2008). "Some Considerations on Command Responsibility and Criminal Liability." *International Review of the Red Cross,* Vol. 90, no. 870 (June 2008), 303–317.

Wilson, Mark (2014). "Moral Grief and Reflective Virtue." *Virtue and the Moral Life: Theological and Philosophical Perspectives.* Eds. William Werpehowski and Kathryn Getek Soltis. Lanham, MD: Lexington Books, 57–73.

Winright, Tobias and E. Ann Jeschke (2015). "Combat and Confession: Just War and Moral Injury." *Can War Be Just in the 21st Century? Ethicists Engage the Tradition.* Eds. Tobias Winright and Laurie Johnston. Maryknoll, NY: Orbis Books, 169–187.

Wood, David (2016). *What Have We Done: The Moral Injury of Our Longest Wars.* New York: Little, Brown and Company, digital edition.

Yandell, Michael (2018). Panelist in "Moral Injury – Implications and Applications for Clinicians, Humanists, and Citizens." 27th Annual International Conference, Association for Practical and Professional Ethics (Chicago, 3 March 2018).

Zahavi, Dan (2014). *Self and Other: Exploring Subjectivity, Empathy, and Shame.* Oxford: Oxford University Press.

Notes

1 The term "soldiers" sometimes refers to only junior enlisted members of an army, but I use it in its more general form to refer to members of any rank. In addition, my points regarding soldiers apply just as well to members of the Air Force, Navy, and Marines, but for brevity's sake I do not explicitly mention airmen, sailors, or marines.

2 US Army Training and Doctrine Command (2017, 4).

3 For many, the seminal text remains Walzer (2015; originally published in 1977). The third category of *jus post bellum* is a more recent one focusing on principles that ought to apply to post-conflict actions, such as peace treaties, war crimes trials, and amnesty policies, among other things. For a recent defense of just war theory in view of realist and pacifist criticisms, as well as an extensive introduction to *jus post bellum*, see Orend (2013). My introduction is meant to be only cursory.

4 Orend (2013, 34).

5 Winright and Jeschke (2015, 186).

6 Biggar (2013, 311).

7 Walzer (2015, 129).

8 Dubik (2016, 3–4).

9 Ibid., 15.

10 Ibid., 21.

11 Ibid., 26.

12 Journalist Tony Dokoupil attributes the term "moral injury" to Mac Bica, a Vietnam veteran and philosophy professor; see Dokoupil (2012, 42).

13 A partial sample: Sjoberg (2013); Dahl (2000); Sylvester (1994); Vetlesen (1994).

14 Sylvester (1994, 95).

15 Sjoberg (2013, 193).

16 Sjoberg (2013, 269–270).

17 French (2017, 263).

18 Ibid.

19 Ibid.

20 Ibid.

21 Sherman (2015, 2021).

22 Sherman (2015, 80).

23 Sherman (2021).

24 Scales (2006).

25 Waldman (2014).

26 Ibid., 2. I use the adjectival form "empathetic" instead of "empathic," but I treat them synonymously.

27 Zahavi (2014, 98).

28 Ibid., 101.

29 See US Army Field Manual (FM) 3–07 *Stability* (2014); FM 3–07.1 *Security Force Assistance* (2009) and the superseding document, Army Techniques Publication (ATP) 3–07.10 *Advising* (2017); US Army Doctrinal Publication (ADP) 6–22 *Army Leadership and the Profession* (2019); FM 6–22 *Leader Development* (2015).

30 The 2006 manual, FM 3–24 *Counterinsurgency,* mentions empathy, but the update *Insurgencies and Countering Insurgencies* of 2014 does not, though it

is implied with its recurrent mention of understanding others' perspectives; for other implicit connections, see ADP 2-0 *Intelligence* (2019), FM 2-0 *Intelligence* (2018), and ATP 2-01.3 *Intelligence Preparation of the Battlefield* (2019); ADP 3-0 *Operations* (2019) and FM 3-0 *Operations* (2017); ADP 5-0, *The Operations Process* (2019); FM 3–13, *Information Operations* (2016).
31 The revision was led by David Petraeus and James Mattis and received significant attention. For example, see Kahl (2007).
32 FM 3–24 (2006 version), 7–2.
33 Ibid., 1–15.
34 ATP 3–07.10, 33–34.
35 Goldie (2002, 195).
36 ADP 6–22, 2–12.
37 ADP 6–22, 2–8. It is also important to note that, given this emphasis of empathy as a component of leadership, it is listed explicitly on the evaluation form for commissioned and noncommissioned officers: DA Form 67-10 series and 2166–9 series, respectively.
38 Wilson (2014, 61).
39 I should note that persons may suffer from both PTSD and moral injury and that they may interact in complicated ways. The importance of distinguishing them lies in the different therapeutic strategies they require.
40 Litz et al. (2009). Moral injury is not unique to veterans, even if they may be vulnerable to a particularly stark form of it or to more occasions for it to occur. In the nursing profession, for example, the notion of "moral distress" is very similar. See Wilkinson (1987). My thanks to E. Ann Jeschke for pointing out this connection.
41 Wood (2016, ch. 1).
42 Shay (1994, 3–4).
43 Ibid.
44 Dallaire (2004).
45 Ibid., 6.
46 Henneberger (2014).
47 Dallaire (2004, 4–5).
48 Shay (1994, 31; footnote 9).
49 Wood (2016, ch. 1).
50 Ibid., ch. 11.
51 Shay (1994, 37). Reiterated in Shay (2014, 183).
52 Shay (1994, 31).
53 For two such accounts, see McGreal (1999) and Power (2001).
54 Shay notes the lack of dehumanization in ancient warring between Greeks and Trojans (1994, 103–115).
55 Dallaire (2004, 6).
56 Dallaire (2002). In this interview (and others), Dallaire took up this concern of dehumanization by asking, "Are all humans human or some more human than others?"
57 This distinction is from McMahan (1996, 88–89).
58 Williamson (2008).
59 Shay (1994, 31; footnote 9).
60 Wood (2016, ch. 1).

61 I use "dilemma" to refer to a "conflict of moral requirements," regardless of how resolvable or intractable the conflict purports to be. I take this phrase from McConnell (2014).
62 Foot (1978).
63 The literature is voluminous; for a summary, one might start with the entries in the *Stanford Encyclopedia of Philosophy* regarding "moral dilemmas," "doing vs. allowing harm," and "doctrine of double effect." These entries contain useful bibliographies. These issues largely stem from discussion of the principle of double effect crafted by Aquinas, which is a prominent consideration of *jus in bello* (see *Summa theologiae* II-II q. 64 a. 7).
64 Wood (2016, ch. 1).
65 Wiinikka-Lydon (2018, 6).
66 I take "moral residue" from Williams (1965).
67 Yandell (2018).
68 Wood (2016, ch. 11).
69 Brough (2007).
70 Coates (2016, 58–59).
71 Shay (2014, 182); Litz et al. (2009).
72 Shay (2014, 184). Shay cites the supporting argument of Nussbaum (1986).
73 As introduced by Williams (2006); see also van Ackeren and Kuhler (2016).
74 Wood (2016, ch. 11).
75 Ibid., ch. 1.
76 Stump (2018, 53).
77 Ibid.
78 Wilson (2014, 58).
79 Wilson summarizes Augustine's arguments for grief as a virtue and connects it with Aquinas' virtue of penance (Ibid., 63–66).
80 Within the US military, there has been a concerted effort in recent years to remove a stigma associated with mental health assistance, and soldiers have more access to this assistance than ever, but overlooking the tragic nature of war persists in the culture, nonetheless. It is also debatable whether the mental health field is the right lens through which to address struggles with grief and guilt. See, for example, Bernard Verkamp's critique of modern therapeutic treatment of guilt in *The Moral Treatment of Returning Warriors in Early Medieval and Modern Times* (Scranton: University of Scranton Press, 1993), 72–85.
81 I draw this scale from Wilson (2014, 67).
82 Wood (2016, ch. 1).
83 Wilson (2014, 61).

2   The Nature of Empathy

For the term "empathy" to warrant our attention, it must meaningfully refer to something. Scholars have applied the term to different phenomena, often in a contradictory fashion, and its popular usage commonly equates it to sympathy or compassion.[1] In a recent introduction to the subject, the authors conclude:

> Given this history of the term 'empathy,' and the multiple uses to which it has been put during its short life, it is not surprising that the contributors to this volume often differ in what they mean by the term. In our view, this does not in any way present a difficulty. We believe that it would not be a good idea, even if it were possible, to attempt to regiment the term into one single meaning.[2]

I find this unsatisfying and untrue. The variety of definitions *does* present a difficulty, it generates much confusion, and it probably contributes to empathy's dismissal instead of its thoughtful consideration. It is important to remain open to the possibility of different kinds of empathy, but the contradictory definitions undermine a meaningful conception of it. As these authors highlight, the term is relatively young, so perhaps conceptual confusion is to be expected. However, it should not be embraced as a fine state.

In this chapter, therefore, I aim to be ecumenical in considering various conceptions of empathy, but also committed to an essence such that the term remains meaningful. Straightaway, with only a brief explanation below, I will distinguish empathy from sympathy and focus my unifying effort on the variety of theories that treat empathy as some kind of understanding of another, and not as care for another. I will not be able to resolve the debates between even these remaining conceptions of empathy. Instead, I will offer only a working definition of empathy in light of the literature and my own intuitions and

DOI: 10.4324/9781003248132-2

analysis. I settle for this provisional definition in order to persist with the overall project of empathy's role in the military profession. By the end of the chapter, I hope to have made the definition clear and reasonable, not utterly convincing.

Empathy is importantly different than sympathy. Empathy is understanding what another thinks or feels, but it is not caring for another's well-being.[3] "Whereas empathy is a form of understanding, sympathy involves care and concern."[4] The two concepts are related; in fact, empathy may prompt and aid sympathetic concern, and sympathy may prompt attempts at an empathetic understanding of another. Conflating the terms is probably more common because of David Hume's and Adam Smith's usage of "sympathy" in their works on moral theory; the phenomena they describe, however, corresponds to what we now call empathy. Specifically, Hume's conception resembles the mirroring of another's emotions in lower-level empathy, while Smith's conception resembles the imaginative perspective-taking in higher-level empathy (both lower- and higher-level empathy are terms that I introduce below).[5] Notably, the term "empathy" did not enter the English language until a century after Hume and Smith, which makes it harder to fault them for the confusion.

Research reinforces the intuition that empathy leads to sympathy, but it also shows that it does not necessarily do so.[6] It can, in fact, inhibit sympathy toward some individuals while promoting it for others, given the ease with which we empathize with members of our own culture or other group and the difficulty we can have in empathizing with those outside of these groups. Thus, empathy can introduce a morally problematic partiality. This concern has fueled some to argue against empathy's presumed contribution to morality.[7] It also highlights the difference between empathy and sympathy.[8]

The Lay of the Land

There are four general schools of thought that regard empathy as an understanding of another, specifically her mental states. These theoretical clusters vary in their details about the understanding that empathy provides and in the methods through which we achieve it. Some define empathy as theoretically inferring another's mental states (known as "theory-theory");[9] others define it as imaginatively simulating another's mental states (known as "simulation theory");[10] still others define it as a theoretically unmediated perception of another's mental states (what I will call "direct perception theory");[11]

and, finally, others define it as comprehending another's mental states through narrative competency (what I will call "narrative theory").[12] Some theorists offer hybrid theories that incorporate elements from different areas. Some accounts are more exclusive than others, ruling out other conceptions as different phenomena in the larger topic of social cognition. Sometimes, rival conceptions are treated as necessary precursors for empathy instead of actual instances of empathy. To set the stage for a working definition, I offer a brief summary of these four schools of thought and the general themes of lower-level empathy and higher-level empathy that one finds within them.

Theory-Theory

Derek Matravers clarifies this curious phrase "theory-theory" by saying "it is the *theory* that we each have a *theory* as to how people work."[13] In navigating our social world, proponents claim that we each construct a folk psychological framework to interpret what others do and what they likely think or feel. This approach to empathy involves one's cognitive reasoning abilities to infer what another's mental states must be, given the other's circumstances, temperament, history, and other relevant knowledge. (Therefore, I also refer to this school of thought as "theoretical inference.") In this account of empathy, all one can do is theoretically consider what it would be like for oneself to be in the other's situation. Another person's mental states are assumed to be inaccessible to oneself in any direct manner. "Most obviously, we do not have direct access to what other people know, want, intend or believe, but must infer these mental states on the basis of what they do and say."[14]

Consider a basic case of empathy in which one person witnesses another person shut a car door and catch his fingers between the door and the car frame. The empathizer naturally winces in virtual pain despite nothing happening to her own finger. Furthermore, she knows that the actual pain is the other's and not her own. Under theory-theory, the empathizer infers that the other is in pain because of the premise that smashed fingers hurt, which has been previously established by her own relevantly similar experiences, or by observing how others have reacted in a painful manner to relevantly similar experiences. To empathize with this victim of the car door is to identify what mental states he is experiencing through observation and reasoning.

In addition to *what* another's instantaneous mental states are, empathy as theoretical inference can reveal more general or enduring mental states that answer (at least partially) *why* another behaves the way he does. With the car door victim, a further empathetic effort might draw the empathizer's attention to the victim's young son and the fact that the son cried out just as the victim was closing the car door. The empathizer surmises that the son's cry distracted the victim at exactly the wrong moment, such that he failed to move his fingers appropriately. The empathizer has seen other parents react immediately to a child's cry, and she applies this knowledge to the case at hand. In this manner, the empathizer has ascertained what mental states the victim is experiencing and has gained at least a limited grasp of why.[15]

Simulation Theory

The development of simulation theory grew out of a concern that the theoretical complexity proposed by theory-theory is untenable in light of a closer look at actual empathetic experiences. When someone winces in pain while witnessing fingers smashed in a car door, the instantaneous reaction and understanding seem to defy the methodical calculations offered by theory-theory. Even the realization that the victim's distraction was due to the cry of his son is a part of the empathizer's more global and simultaneous perception of the victim's situation than an act of deliberate reflection. Some theory-theorists respond by saying this deliberation is honed and habituated in most humans to a level of instinctual speed, but simulation theorists maintain that something else must be going on to overcome the inaccessibility of another's mental states. While theoretical inference may corroborate empathetic efforts, simulation theorists argue that its role is secondary and cannot explain empathy itself.[16] In addition, simulation theorists criticize theory-theory for its poor fit with developmental psychology. Children exhibit an understanding of others' mental states in infancy, yet at that same age, they are incapable of the theoretical reasoning required by theory-theory.[17]

Instead, proponents of simulation theory argue for a different conception of cognitive abilities to overcome the inaccessibility of another's mental states: simulating another's circumstances in one's own mind. Amy Coplan defines empathy as an "imaginative process in which an observer simulates another person's situated psychological states while maintaining clear self-other differentiation."[18] In simulating another's situation, the empathizer not only imagines being in the other's circumstances, but, importantly, imagines being *the other* in those circumstances. This "other-oriented perspective-taking" achieves an empathetic understanding far more reliably than "self-oriented perspective-taking."[19] It is this kind of imaginative effort that produces the empathizer's understanding of the car door victim's pain and his distraction by his son (an understanding of both *what* and *why*), not the overtly inferential effort of theory-theory. Furthermore, in imagining the other in his circumstances, the empathizer runs them through her own mental framework "offline," as compared to the full "online" engagement with her own circumstances.[20] Thus, offline simulation is seen to overcome the challenge to theory-theory of overly deliberative reflection. It also connects with the intuition that empathy is not purely theoretical; it is less of a "cold affair, [different than] the way we understand how an airplane flies. Empathy requires first of all emotional engagement."[21] Mentally simulating another's circumstances more readily accounts for the holistic combination of affective and cognitive components in the other's experience.

Simulation theory arguably received a significant boost with recent neuroscientific discoveries. Beginning in the 1990s, scientists observed that certain neurons in the brain fired not only when a subject performed a certain action, but when the subject observed that same action in another.[22] Even though the subject's neuron activity matched that of the one observed, the subject did not perform the same action. There was "mental mimicry" but not "behavioral mimicry."[23] This mental mirroring led to the label of "mirror" neurons, and specific types of mirror neurons have been associated with behavior, sounds, and emotions.[24] The research has radically changed theories concerning child development. A few decades ago, the consensus was that infants were "asocial and egocentric," becoming socially aware in later stages of development. Now, infants are believed to have certain basic social capacities from birth, such as imitation and intersubjective communication.[25] In general, the mirror neuron system is seen to reveal the plans or intentions of others, and thus, provides at least a limited means to overcome the inaccessibility of other minds. Many see the discovery of the mirror neuron system as a promising empirical basis for the concept of offline simulation.

Direct Perception Theory

Some philosophers, however, resist the above schools of thought out of a concern that they miss the other-centered character of empathy. Drawing on phenomenological accounts of empathy by Edith Stein, Edmund Husserl, Max Scheler, and Alfred Schutz, Dan Zahavi argues that theory-theory and simulation theory fall prey to an "egocentric predicament," since they artificially restrict the phenomenon of empathy to what we might attribute to others from our own experience.[26] Neither conception, in his view, accounts for the basic fact of being able to directly perceive the mental states of others. When the empathizer witnesses the father's fingers crunched in the car door, the pain is more immediately available to her than either theoretically inferring it or simulating it. "I experience rather than imagine or infer my friend's distress."[27] Empathy is not a conjecture about another's mental states, as if they were "unobservable, theoretical posits," but a perception of mental states in one's experience of the other.[28] Zahavi thinks that this error of projecting mental states onto the other in the more cognitively complex accounts undermines them as proper descriptions of empathy. Instead, Zahavi defines empathy as a "perceptually based and theoretically unmediated experience of the other."[29]

The direct perception account does not assume an "epistemological gap" between the input one receives by attending to another and the output of the other's mental states, as in theoretical inferencing and simulation.[30] Theory-theory suggests that this gap is overcome through conscious deliberation; simulation theory suggests that it is overcome by sub-personal processes of offline simulation. The proposal of direct perception, however, is simply that this gap is not present. Empathy is the *theoretically unmediated* perception of another's mental states; we perceive another's pain, or anger, or joy, like we perceive a lemon.[31] It is the other's mental state "itself that I am facing, there is nothing that gets in the way, and the state is experienced as actually present to me. This is precisely what distinguishes empathy from other, more indirect forms of social cognition."[32] Under the theory of direct perception, then, the inaccessibility of other minds is a false assumption.

More precisely, the assumption is greatly exaggerated. While Zahavi maintains that empathy uniquely reveals various "surface attitudes" of an affective or cognitive nature, he does not think it provides "an especially profound or deep kind of understanding. In order to obtain that, theoretical inferences and imaginative simulations might very well be needed."[33] In other words, conceiving of empathy as direct perception restricts it to providing the *what* of another's experience, but not the *why* behind it. For Zahavi, the empathizer's wincing in pain at the car door victim's injury counts as empathy; the further realization that the son's cry distracted the victim does not.

Zahavi thinks the discovery of mirror neurons is important, but he remains wary of the claims made in light of it. Mirror neuron researchers often say that mirror neurons allow "direct experiential understanding of others," yet also speak of mirror neurons enabling an inner imitation that allows the empathizer to discern the meaning of others' actions (the *why* instead of just the *what*).[34] Zahavi finds a tension here, since only the former stance seems to take seriously the phenomenological point about the givenness of the other's experience. With imitation, the empathizer projects meaning instead of receiving it (or maintaining it as unknown). Furthermore, Zahavi warns we must be precise with what mirror neurons actually provide. They may help "decode another agent's motor intentions, [but] they cannot help us to determine his or her prior intentions."[35] It is overly ambitious to claim mirror neurons reveal the meaning behind some behavior, even if they plausibly convey the person's particular mental states at that moment.

Narrative Theory

Zahavi's projective concern is an important challenge to theory-theory and simulation theory, but some think that Zahavi risks an error in the other direction by limiting empathy to only that which is directly perceived in face-to-face encounters. Shaun Gallagher, for example, offers a phenomenologically informed concept of "direct social perception" that closely resembles Zahavi's theoretically unmediated perception.[36] However, Gallagher maintains empathy as something more than this perceptual act, something that requires an understanding of "the context of the other, where context means more than perceptual context and includes historical and cultural aspects."[37] When we empathize, Gallagher suggests that we aspire to the meaning behind the other's actions, not just the other's current mental states. Empathy refers to something that is more of an achievement than it is a default, automatic, and largely subconscious perception.[38]

Gallagher, therefore, crafts his definition of empathy with an emphasis on understanding the *why* instead of merely the *what*. He argues that our employment of narrative frameworks is the best explanation for how we empathetically understand others:

> [Narratives] give us a form or structure that we can use in understanding others. That is, we learn from narrative how to frame an understanding of others. We start to see others engaged in their actions, not simply in terms of the immediate and occurrent context. We start to see them as engaged in longer-term projects (plots) that add meaning to what they are doing.[39]

that rule this out. In fact, recent neuroscientific research indicates that different parts of the brain engage when taking on a self- vs. other-oriented perspective, providing some empirical basis for this possibility.[61]

Given that both lower-level and higher-level empathy are compatible with this working definition, I will include both. I share Zahavi's projective concern with higher-level processes, but I also share the intuition of Gallagher and others that empathy refers to an achievement that is something more than a shallow understanding of another's surface mental states.

Integrating Lower- and Higher-level Empathy

In line with Stueber, I propose that we consider empathy as a perception-like faculty in which higher-level empathetic abilities build on lower-level empathetic input. Conceiving of lower-level empathetic processes as akin to sensory input is already present in the accounts of Zahavi, Stueber, Gallagher, and Coplan (though, to be precise, the latter two want to restrict the term "empathy" to higher-level processes).[62] Furthermore, the idea of empathy as the combination of raw sensory input plus higher cognitive processing can help to illustrate how they complement each other, as well as how the empathetic endeavor can go wrong.

On the one hand, lower-level empathy unrefined by higher-level empathy can result in knowing less than what could be known. The empathizer would only perceive the other's immediate mental states with no appreciation for the *why* behind his behavior. It would be similar to the error of raw visual input with no higher cognitive processing – seeing color and shape but not piecing together the image to conclude *tree*. Admittedly, there may be some rudimentary interpretation built into lower-level empathy; Zahavi notes the philosophical work that establishes the sub-personal interpretation of context that occurs in visual perception.[63] However, this does not do justice to the contributions that higher-level processes make in understanding the full meaning of another's experience.

Conversely, higher-level empathy unanchored by lower-level empathetic input can result in the error of projection that motivates Zahavi's critique of theory-theory and simulation theory. If not corrected by the perceptual act of lower-level empathy (as enabled, perhaps, by the mirror neuron system) the imaginative work of higher-level empathy is free to draw conclusions about the other's mental states based solely on assumptions about the other, or based on the empathizer's own experiences, values, intentions, or prejudices. In Coplan's words, "we don't just fail to understand others' subjective experiences; we often assume that we do understand them, which leads to a new set of problems."[64] It would be similar to the error of cognitive processing overriding raw visual input, which, when taken to an extreme, is a moment of hallucination, "a seemingly real perception of something not actually present."[65] When higher cognitive effort at empathizing with another is not tethered by a receptive mode toward the other's actual experience, it risks turning into a presumptuous and self-deceiving exercise.

Taken as a cohesive whole, lower- and higher-level empathy each contribute to the achievement of understanding the other's experience in its synergy of cognitive states, affective states, and specific circumstances.

What Empathy Provides

There is a crucial epistemic upshot to empathy. It offers what "no third-person form of scientific understanding can: understanding of another person from the 'inside';" this inside view is an "experiential understanding...of another person's thoughts, feelings, and behavior."[66] It is an understanding of another's lived experience. Cultural anthropologists distinguish between an "emic" and an "etic" understanding, where "emic" refers to the meanings and interpretations that drive behavior and "etic" refers to only the observable behavior itself.[67] The physical sciences aim solely for an etic understanding of their inanimate subjects; there is no sense in a chemist seeking an emic understanding of molecules. The subject matter of physical science lends itself to explanation through causal relationships derived from observable behavior. When accurate, these explanations offer a great amount of certainty and predictive power. In the social sciences, on the other hand, practitioners seek greater understanding of "the meaning of actions," the impetus behind decisions, which yields less certainty and predictability.[68] Unlike the chemist, the psychologist and anthropologist study "molecules with minds of their own."[69] Empathy is inherent to the practice of the social sciences insofar as they aim for this inside knowledge instead of strict causal principles, which human nature persistently defies.[70] As Stueber concludes, "empathy must be regarded as of central epistemic importance and as the epistemic default mode in understanding other agents."[71]

This distinction between etic and emic understanding is similar to Eleonore Stump's difference between "knowledge that" and "knowledge of." Stump draws a correspondence to left-brain and right-brain skills, respectively. The precision and analytic detail associated with the left hemisphere of the brain lend themselves to propositional knowledge, while the breadth of focus and capacity for narrative associated with the right hemisphere is better for interpersonal knowledge.[72] The difference shows up in the contrast between "knowing about Andrew" vs. simply "knowing Andrew," or "what I know about Iraqis" vs. "the Iraqis I know." Stump argues that both types of knowledge are important and that neither are reducible to the other, though propositional knowledge is by far the most common in philosophical discourse. This predisposition becomes most pronounced when humans are involved. Stump notes, "The deficit will perhaps be undetectable in work on modal logic or philosophy of mathematics, but in any issues where the interactions of persons make a difference it is more likely to be in evidence."[73]

This deficit is clearly visible in the study and practice of war. Military professionals have often approached war as natural scientists, treating the subject as inert and requiring only a sufficient level of etic understanding to achieve victory. An extreme example is the work of Adam Heinrich Dietrich von Bulow, a Prussian military theorist who claimed to have reduced military strategy to a geometrical science involving the lines of operation between attacker and defender.[74] A less extreme example, but one that nevertheless displays the same deficit, is the US military's investment in cultural knowledge over the last twenty years.

Once the conventional conflict against the Iraqi army ended in the summer of 2003, the military was faced with the more interpersonal challenge of establishing security and fostering a new regime in Iraq (paralleling the effort in Afghanistan). In the ensuing years, each branch of the military established cultural centers of expertise, mandated culture awareness training, increased incentives for fluency in foreign languages, and revised the curricula of professional education to better address cultural matters.[75] The most public and controversial effort involved hiring anthropologists and sociologists to embed with military units and provide commanders cultural expertise.[76] However, this investment in largely propositional knowledge about the Iraqi and Afghan cultures provided only meager improvement in the ability to persuade, influence, and win the cooperation of the populations. Military personnel remained ill-prepared to take on persuasion in the wake of coercion, or more accurately, to weave the right mix of these into operational plans.

Empathy is the key element that shifts one from merely being aware of another culture's features to being "competent" in that culture.[77] Empathy balances the military's customary predisposition for an etic understanding with the vital insights of an emic understanding. As Carl von Clausewitz (another Prussian military theorist) states:

> [the] essential difference is that war is not an exercise of the will directed at inanimate matter …. [It] is clear that continual striving after laws analogous to those appropriate to the realm of inanimate matter was bound to lead to one mistake after another.[78]

An etic understanding of war is necessary given inanimate elements like terrain, weather, and weapon ranges; but this understanding is insufficient by itself. Military personnel also require an emic understanding that accommodates the human element. Empathy helps to attain that emic understanding and employ cultural knowledge not as simplistic rules of behavior, but as the foundation for grasping another person's unique sense-making.

Empathy Can Promote Objectivity

It might sound counterintuitive, but given the clearer notion of empathy above, it should be apparent how empathy generally improves critical thinking and gaining an even-handed view on a topic. To illustrate briefly, consider the three fallacies of naïve realism, false consensus effect, and confirmation bias.

Naïve realism is the error of assuming one has the singular objective stance on something.[79] When discovering a different opinion, the naïve realist concludes that the other party is either responding to different information, is lazy or irrational, or is biased due to ideology or self-interest.[80] In the case of simply different information, the naïve realist further anticipates reaching full agreement once the difference is sorted out. She does not recognize the possibility of competing conclusions from the same facts. She believes her approach to be the only one possible. An empathetic understanding serves as an antidote to this illogical, sometimes arrogant, error. Not only does it foster consideration of alternative interpretations of facts, but it also promotes respect for others that makes it harder to rashly accuse someone of ideological or selfish bias.

The false consensus effect is a softer version of naïve realism. While a person may not insist others are wrongheaded like the naïve realist, he may incorrectly assume a consensus when group members are merely being silent. The leader may want consensus badly enough that he is too quick to claim it, overestimating the agreement of others.[81] An empathetic understanding of group members helps in anticipating their objections. If someone fails to offer some expected counterpoint, the leader can find out why instead of taking the silence as agreement.

Confirmation bias is the error of favoring evidence that supports a preferred hypothesis while ignoring contrary evidence.[82] It can occur in the collection or the interpretation of evidence. This fallacy is a greater risk the stronger a person prefers one outcome over another. Extreme confidence can also increase the risk, since the person will tend to ignore her own fallibility. John Stuart Mill has this overly confident person in mind when he warns:

> [W]hile everyone well knows himself to be fallible, few think it necessary to take any precautions against their own fallibility, or admit the supposition that any opinion, of which they feel very certain, may be one of the examples of the error to which they acknowledge themselves to be liable.[83]

Empathy helps a person operationalize Mill's advice, shifting the recognition of one's own fallibility from merely an ethereal concept to a practical, concrete reality. Empathizing with others invariably produces claims that contradict one's own; the understanding stemming from that act of empathy helps one carefully consider the contrary claim instead of hastily dismissing it. One can also better imagine alternative interpretations of data.

Admittedly, an empathetic understanding may also invite certain fallacies. Empathetic error is something like the inverse of observer bias in the natural sciences: instead of the observer's actions interfering with what is being observed, the empathizer's actions interfere with her own affective or cognitive states. Again, three brief examples:

Over-identification is traditionally a concern of anthropologists or psychologists in which an observer immerses herself so much in the subject's experience that she cannot distinguish it from her own or cannot objectively evaluate it.[84] "Going native" is the colloquial label, though this may refer to identifying with another culture or worldview rather than a specific person. The "inside" knowledge, especially of the subject's affective state, dominates the observer's view and causes a loss of analytical ability.

Naïve fallibility is the opposite of naïve realism above. Instead of assuming oneself is singularly right, the naïve fallibilist assumes he always has the faulty opinion about something, deferring too much to the opinions of others.[85] Seeking an empathetic understanding risks this error because the empathizer suspends judgment in order to understand another's perspective. Instead of reengaging his own judgment to see if he agrees with that perspective, he simply adopts the other's opinion as his own. This error is more likely if the empathizer lacks confidence regarding the topic at hand. It can also stem from a desire to avoid conflict, accepting the other's opinion merely to maintain the peace.

Lastly, an empathetic understanding does not necessarily avoid the fallacy of hasty generalization. The insights about one individual or subgroup might be wrongly applied to the larger group.[86] Empathy can be difficult enough to accomplish that it is tempting to generalize instead of repeating the process with other group members. The empathizer may commit this error accidentally; she may not be aware of distinctions within the group. (Seeking an empathetic understanding can itself help prevent this error: empathizing with a group member can reveal those distinctions within the group that the observer originally did not see.)

Conclusion

Achieving empathy is harder than it may first appear, as Gallagher underscores in his work. We are swayed by our own emotional capacity and the phenomenality of our own experience. In attributing mental states to another, we easily and unconsciously presume that another's experience will mimic our own. We may even stubbornly resist the possibility of a different phenomenality than what we have correlated to the same kind of circumstances. Empathy, however, entails an appreciative understanding that recognizes the validity of the other's experience as genuine even if not the same as ours. Being empathetic does not require agreeing with the other's perspective or adopting the other's perspective as our own, but it does require recognizing the other's authority regarding his own experience. We are not free to dismiss the other's experience as incomprehensible or impossible, because its possibility is being instantiated in the other person and empathy reveals the person's experience to us.

There is, therefore, always a thread of solidarity between empathizer and target in some kind of shared human nature or shared conditions for the possibility of experience. This shared human condition enables both a minimal degree of solidarity and a minimal degree of empathy, despite great socio-cultural differences. Beyond this foundational solidarity, however, the myriad differences with the other take over, and the correspondence of solidarity and empathy falls away. The understanding of how another feels or thinks becomes pointedly distinct from identifying with how another feels or thinks.

To empathize is to expose oneself to a kind of vulnerability. Seeking an empathetic understanding of another's experience means subjecting oneself to its affective character. This aspect may be unfamiliar, unpleasant, uncomfortable, inconvenient, or painful. It can also be unnerving and possibly damaging in some way. In empathetically considering the immoral behavior of others, Stump writes,

> The mirror neuron system [underlying empathy] gives the viewer some no doubt limited sense of what it feels like to do such things and to want to do them, even though it gives this sense in a way disconnected from the viewer's own intellect and will. Sensing what it feels like to do and to want to do such things can be very troubling if the things in question are deeply revulsive to one's moral sensibilities, to one's own beliefs and desires.[87]

So it is understandable that we sometimes resist empathy.[88] Indeed, there are circumstances where avoiding the affective character of another's experience is commendable; in a hospital's emergency room, for example, medical staff need to carefully manage "emotional engagement" with patients' injuries that might otherwise overwhelm their judgment with empathetic pain.[89] The medical staff remain obligated to recognizing what their patients feel and respecting the validity of that experience, even if they rightly avoid taking in the affective character of that experience. These moments of avoiding an empathetic understanding are temporary interruptions to their automatic lower-level empathy produced by the mirror neuron system. As Frans de Waal observes, the "automaticity" of mirror neurons does not mean lack of control: "My breathing, for instance, is fully automated, yet I remain in charge."[90] Or, it is like the faculty of seeing or hearing, whose exercise is generally automatic, with only occasional exceptions to shade one's eyes and avoid looking directly at the sun or to wear earplugs and avoid exposure to harmful levels of sound. The medical staff's need to interrupt empathy, however, must be temporary due to the need for empathetic understanding and their other need to process pent-up emotions that are inextricably linked to their care of patients.

These limited exceptions aside, empathy is good to achieve because it is an expression of recognition respect (in this manner, empathy is an end in itself) and because it reveals the experience of others (empathy's instrumental value). Our motivations, attitudes, values, feelings, desires, perspectives, and commitments govern our behavior. Empathy, therefore, is an essential type of knowledge to comprehend others and their actions.

Works Cited

Abbe, Allison and Stanley M. Halpin (2009). "The Cultural Imperative for Professional Military Education and Leader Development." *Parameters*, Vol. 39, no. 4, 20–31.

Apperly, Ian (2011). *Mindreaders: The Cognitive Basis of "Theory of Mind."* New York: Psychology Press.

Batson, C. Daniel (2009). "These Things Called Empathy." *The Social Neuroscience of Empathy.* Eds. Jean Decety and William Ickes. Cambridge, MA: MIT Press, 3–15.

Batson, C. Daniel (1991). *The Altruism Question: Toward a Social-psychological Answer.* Hillsdale, NJ: Erlbaum.

Bloom, Paul (2016). *Against Empathy.* New York: HarperCollins.

Bohl, Vivian and Nivedita Gangopadhyay (2013). "Theory of Mind and the Unobservability of Other Minds." *Philosophical Explorations*, Vol. 17, no. 2, 203–222.

Clausewitz, Carl von (1832). *On War.* Trans. Michael Howard and Peter Paret. Princeton, NJ: Princeton University Press (1976).

Coates, A.J. (2016). *The Ethics of War.* 2nd ed. Manchester: Manchester University Press.

Coplan, Amy (2011). "Understanding Empathy: Its Features and Effects." *Empathy: Philosophical and Psychological Perspectives.* Eds. Amy Coplan and Peter Goldie. New York: Oxford University Press, 3–18.

Coplan, Amy and Peter Goldie (2011). "Introduction." *Empathy: Philosophical and Psychological Perspectives.* Eds. Amy Coplan and Peter Goldie. New York: Oxford University Press, ix–xlvii.

Darwall, Stephen (2009). *The Second-Person Standpoint: Morality, Respect, and Accountability.* Cambridge, MA: Harvard University Press.

Darwall, Stephen (1998). "Empathy, Sympathy, and Care." *Philosophical Studies*, Vol. 89, 261–282.

de Waal, Frans (2009). *The Age of Empathy: Nature's Lessons for a Kinder Society.* New York: Three Rivers Press.

Decety, Jean and Andrew Meltzoff (2011). "Empathy, Imitation, and the Social Brain." *Empathy: Philosophical and Psychological Perspectives.* Eds. Amy Coplan and Peter Goldie. New York: Oxford University Press, 58–81.

DeWalt, Kathleen and Billie DeWalt (2011). *Participant-Observation: A Guide for Fieldworkers.* 2nd ed. Lanham, MD: AltaMira Press.

Fogassi, Leonardo and Vittorio Gallese (2002). "The Neural Correlates of Action Understanding in Non-human Primates." *Mirror Neurons and the*

Evolution of Brain and Language. Eds. Vittorio Gallese and Maksim Stamenov. Philadelphia: John Benjamins Publishing, 13–35.

Gaddis, John Lewis (2002). *The Landscape of History: How Historians Map the Past.* New York: Oxford University Press.

Gallagher, Shaun (2015). "The New Hybrids: Continuing Debates on Social Perception." *Consciousness and Cognition,* Vol. 36, 452–465.

Gallagher, Shaun (2012). "Empathy, Simulation, and Narrative." *Science in Context,* Vol. 25, no. 3, 355–381.

Gat, Azar (2001). *A History of Military Thought: From the Enlightenment to the Cold War.* New York: Oxford University Press.

Goldie, Peter (2011). "Anti-Empathy." *Empathy: Philosophical and Psychological Perspectives.* Eds. Amy Coplan and Peter Goldie. New York: Oxford University Press, 302–317.

Goldie, Peter (2000). *The Emotions: a Philosophical Exploration.* Oxford: Oxford University Press.

Goldman, Alvin (2011). "Two Routes to Empathy." *Empathy: Philosophical and Psychological Perspectives.* Eds. Amy Coplan and Peter Goldie. New York: Oxford University Press, 31–44.

Goldman, Alvin (2006). *Simulating Minds: The Philosophy, Psychology, and Neuroscience of Mindreading.* Oxford: Oxford University Press.

Hutto, Daniel (2008). *Folk Psychological Narratives: The Socio-Cultural Basis of Understanding Reasons.* Cambridge, MA: MIT Press.

Ickes, William (2003). *Everyday Mind Reading: Understanding What Other People Think and Feel.* Amherst, NY: Prometheus Books.

Jaschik, Scott (2015). "Embedded Conflicts." *Inside Higher Ed.* (7 July 2015). <https://www.insidehighered.com/news/2015/07/07/army-shuts-down-controversial-human-terrain-system-criticized-many-anthropologists>.

Kassel, Whitney (2015). "The Army Needs Anthropologists." *Foreign Policy* (28 July 2015). <http://foreignpolicy.com/2015/07/28/ the-army-needs-anthropologists-iraq-afghanistan-human-terrain/>.

Lamm, Claus, C. Daniel Batson, and Jean Decety (2007). "The Neural Substrate of Human Empathy: Effects of Perspective Taking and Cognitive Appraisal." *Journal of Cognitive Neuroscience,* Vol. 19, no. 1, 42–58.

Lanzoni, Susan (2018). *Empathy: A History.* New Haven: Yale University Press.

Lavenda, Robert H. and Emily A. Schultz (2007). *Core Concepts in Cultural Anthropology.* 3rd ed. Boston: McGraw-Hill.

Maibom, Heidi (2014). "Introduction." *Empathy and Morality.* Ed. Heidi Maibom. Oxford: Oxford University Press, 1–40.

Matravers, Derek (2017). *Empathy.* Malden, MA: Polity Press.

Mill, John Stuart (1859). *On Liberty.* Project Gutenberg eBook version. <https://www.gutenberg.org/files/34901/34901-h/34901-h.htm>.

Moore, Don (2007). "Not So Above Average After All: When People Believe They Are Worse than Average and Its Implications for Theories of Bias in Social Comparison." *Organizational Behavior and Human Decision Processes*, Vol. 102 (January 2007), 42–58.

Munson, Ronald and Andrew Black (2007). *The Elements of Reasoning.* 5th ed. Belmont, CA: Thomson Wadsworth.

Nickerson, Raymond (1998). "Confirmation Bias: A Ubiquitous Phenomenon in Many Guises." *Review of General Psychology*, Vol. 2, no. 2, 175–220.

Prinz, Jesse (2011). "Is Empathy Necessary for Morality?" *Empathy: Philosophical and Psychological Perspectives.* Eds. Amy Coplan and Peter Goldie. New York: Oxford University Press, 211–229.

Reid, Thomas (1872). *The Works of Thomas Reid, Vol. 1.* Elibron Classics Replica Edition (facsimile of original 1872 edition). Ed. William Hamilton. Chestnut Hill, MA: Adamant Media Corporation (2005).

Ross, Lee and Andrew Ward (1995). "Naïve Realism: Implications for Social Conflict and Misunderstanding." Stanford Center on Conflict and Negotiation, Working Paper No. 48 (May 1995).

Ross, Lee, David Greene, and Pamela House (1977). "The False Consensus Effect: An Egocentric Bias in Social Perception and Attribution Processes." *Journal of Experimental Social Psychology*, Vol. 13, no. 3, 279–301.

Smith, Joel (2015). "What Is Empathy For?" *Synthese*, Vol. 194, 709–722.

Stueber, Karsten (2006). *Rediscovering Empathy: Agency, Folk Psychology, and the Human Sciences.* Cambridge, MA: MIT Press.

Stump, Eleonore (2018). *Atonement.* Oxford: Oxford University Press.

Stump, Eleonore (2010). *Wandering in Darkness: Narrative and the Problem of Suffering.* Oxford: Oxford University Press.

US Army Field Manual 3-24.2 *Tactics in Counterinsurgency.* Fort Leavenworth: Combined Arms Doctrine Directorate, 2009.

Zahavi, Dan (2014). *Self and Other: Exploring Subjectivity, Empathy, and Shame.* New York: Oxford University Press.

Notes

1 See Batson (2009) for an illustrative summary; for fuller introductions of the term and its history, see Stueber (2006); Coplan and Goldie (2011); Zahavi (2014); Matravers (2017); and Lanzoni (2018).
2 Coplan and Goldie (2011, xxxi).
3 Darwall (1998, 261–270). Note that I mean "care" in a strong sense. As Shaun Gallagher notes, one might care in a weak sense, meaning just being attentive to the person, but not being intent on the person's flourishing, and thus, not counting as a moment of sympathy. Care in this weak sense is, however, part of empathy. See Gallagher (2012, 362).
4 As paraphrased by Zahavi (2014, 139; footnote 14).
5 Darwall (1998, 267); Coplan and Goldie (2011, x).
6 Batson (1991); Darwall (1998, 272–273).
7 Prinz (2011); Bloom (2016).
8 For more extensive discussion on the relationship between empathy and sympathy, see Darwall (1998); Coplan and Goldie (2011, x–xi); Gallagher (2012, 360–362); Zahavi (2014, 115–117); Matravers (2017, 115).

9 Such as Ickes (2003) and Apperly (2011).
10 Such as Goldman (2006); Stueber (2006); Coplan (2011); and Matravers (2017).
11 Such as Edith Stein, Edmund Husserl, Max Scheler, and Alfred Schutz, as summarized and extended by Zahavi (2014, 115–191).
12 Such as Gallagher (2012) and Hutto (2008).
13 Matravers (2017, 26).
14 Apperly (2011, 1). See also Bohl and Gangopadhyay (2013).
15 I take this distinction of *what* and *why* from Zahavi (2014, 167).
16 See Stueber (2006, 21).
17 Decety and Meltzoff (2011).
18 Coplan (2011, 5).
19 Ibid., 9–15. Coplan notes that self-oriented perspective-taking can provide an empathetic understanding when "there is a great deal of overlap between self and other or where the situation is the type that would lead to a fairly universal response" (9). For a criticism of the possibility of other-oriented perspective-taking, see Goldie (2011).
20 I take this contrast of "offline" and "online" from Darwall (1998, 271) and Stump (2018).
21 de Waal (2009, 72).
22 Fogassi and Gallese (2002, 14–19).
23 Goldman (2011, 34).
24 Coplan and Goldie (2011, xxix–xxx).
25 Decety and Meltzoff (2011).
26 Zahavi (2014, 110).
27 Ibid., 126.
28 Ibid., 154.
29 Ibid., 98.
30 Ibid., 175.
31 Ibid., 98, 178.
32 Ibid., 180.
33 Ibid., 142, 151.
34 Ibid., 160.
35 Ibid., 159.
36 Gallagher (2015, 452).
37 Gallagher (2012, 377), particularly endnote 11.
38 Ibid., 358: "saying that I empathize with you, seems to suggest more than just understanding your mental state; it seems to mean more than simply perceiving that you are in pain, even if this perception is informed by an embodied resonance."
39 Ibid., 371. Daniel Hutto offers a similar narrative account (2008). Peter Goldie says empathy is when a person "centrally imagines the narrative (the thoughts, feelings, and emotions) of another person" (2000, 195). I lack the space to consider how Goldie's use of the imagination is different from Gallagher's use of narrative competency. Presumably, though, Gallagher would defend narrative competency as less conscious and cognitively complex than Goldie's imaginative effort, as well as more capable of avoiding Zahavi's projective concern.
40 Ibid., 372.
41 Coplan and Goldie (2011, xxxiii).

42 Besides the references already cited, see Stueber (2006, 131–151) and Matravers (2017, 52–61).
43 Coplan (2011, 5).
44 Stueber (2006); Goldman (2011).
45 Stueber (2006, 20).
46 Zahavi (2014, 118–125).
47 Stueber (2006, 147).
48 Ibid., 21.
49 Ibid.
50 Smith (2015, 711).
51 It is important to also note that the accuracy of empathizing increases with one's knowledge about one's friend – whether she is naturally optimistic, or worrisome, etc. This acquaintance can give greater fidelity to the empathetic attempt to understand the friend's experience.
52 As cited by Zahavi (2014, 118).
53 Smith (2015, 712–713).
54 Heidi Maibom does not require attribution in her notion of "affective empathy" (2014, 2–5); nor does Alvin Goldman in his conception of mirroring (2011, 33).
55 Goldman (2011, 34).
56 Ibid. For other statements of this attribution condition, see Stueber (2006, 20); Coplan (2011, 5); Gallagher (2012, 358); Zahavi (2014, 189); and Matravers (2017, 76).
57 Darwall (2009, 122–123).
58 Coplan (2011), Goldie (2000).
59 Gallagher (2012), Hutto (2008).
60 Coplan (2011, 15).
61 Lamm et al. (2007).
62 This comparison is also motivated by Thomas Reid's observation that our ability to detect the emotions and intentions of others is "very analogous to that of the external senses" (Reid 1872, 450).
63 Zahavi (2014, 163–164).
64 Coplan (2011, 11–12).
65 Oxford English Dictionary.
66 Coplan (2011, 17, 18).
67 Lavenda and Schultz (2007, 43).
68 Coplan and Goldie (2011, xv–xvi). This "meaning of actions" also corresponds to the concept of *verstehen* in the philosophy of social science (see Stueber 2006, 13–16).
69 Gaddis (2002, 111).
70 Stueber (2006, 13).
71 Ibid., 219.
72 Stump (2010, 23–25).
73 Ibid., 25.
74 Gat (2001, 81–96).
75 Abbe and Halpin (2010, 20–31).
76 The American Anthropological Association opposed the program (called the Human Terrain System) as a violation of the profession's ethics. See Jaschik (2015). For an argument in favor of the concept but critical of this program, see Kassel (2015).

77 I take this idea from US Army Field Manual 3-24.2 *Tactics in Counterinsurgency* (2009), which states: "Empathy leads to Cultural Competence: truly understanding other human beings and where they come from allows honest relationships to develop" (p. 8-21).

78 Clausewitz (1832, 149).

79 I mean the cognitive error discussed in social psychology, not the direct perception of objects in the philosophy of mind.

80 Ross and Ward (1995, 110–111).

81 The term "false consensus effect" derives from Ross et al. (1977).

82 Nickerson (1998).

83 Mill (1859, ch. 2).

84 DeWalt and DeWalt (2011, 6, 22).

85 The term "naïve fallibility" is my own. The closest fallacy I could find is the worse-than-average effect, which is the tendency of some persons who are poor at a given task to underestimate their performance of that task in relation to others (despite being poor, they may yet perform the task better than others). Naïve fallibility refers to a more general predisposition toward another's superior reasoning, regardless of one's own reasoning ability. For the worse-than-average effect, see Moore (2007).

86 Munson and Black (2007, 141).

87 Stump (2018, 160).

88 See Matravers (2017, 91–94), for further consideration of this hesitation to empathize.

89 de Waal (2009, 72).

90 Ibid., 79.

3 Empathy and *Jus in bello*

Parallel to investigating the nature of empathy, one must get at the nature of soldiering in order to determine if the two are compatible. The question is whether empathy is detrimental to a soldier's duties. I intend to show that empathy is actually crucial, since empathy helps to fulfill the moral principles of *jus in bello*. Empathy's biggest contribution is bolstering the principle of right intention by interrupting the dehumanizing tendencies common to war. This right intention is further manifested in the war-fighting responsibilities of discrimination and proportionality, as well as the war-waging responsibilities of strategic planning and assessment.

The Neglect of Right Intention

The principle of right intention is "the appropriate disposition of those [individuals] fighting wars" toward a just and lasting peace.[1] Early just war theorists emphasized right intention as essential to the moral warrant for war and to soldiers' conduct in it.[2] The principle is meant to serve as a correction for statesmen or soldiers who may have a justified cause for war, but use that cause merely as a screen for other purposes. As modern thinkers drew brighter lines between *jus ad bellum* and *jus in bello* (and eventually *jus post bellum*), right intention only appeared in the *ad bellum* category. Presumably, it could still influence *in bello* considerations by its presence in the deliberations precipitating war. However, right intention has received circumspect attention in modern discussions of *jus ad bellum*.[3] Some scholars have since suggested that right intention is redundant or impossible to corroborate and should be subsumed under the principle of just cause.[4]

Others have focused on laws and rules to externally restrain politicians and soldiers, shifting away from intentions and virtues that might internally restrain them.[5] A.J. Coates contrasts this trend

DOI: 10.4324/9781003248132-3

toward a "rule-based approach" with a more traditional "charac-ter-based approach."[6] While he recognizes merits in both, he finds in the rule-based approach an antagonism toward the charac-ter-based approach. The rule-based approach prioritizes delibera-tive reflection about moral demands at the exclusion of dispositional considerations:

> 'Reflective' morality is not just neglectful of, or indifferent to-wards, the idea of a moral life centred on moral dispositions, it is opposed to it on principle, since 'the mind without disposition is alone the spring of "rational" judgement and "rational" con-duct.' Moral conduct is 'rational' in the narrowly conceived sense of 'conduct springing from an antecedent process of "reasoning,"' excluding conduct which has its source in 'the unexamined au-thority of a tradition, a custom or a habit of behavior.' From a reflective standpoint, the communal and habitual aspects of tra-ditional morality are seen less as sources of moral empowerment than as fundamental obstacles to the achievement of moral au-tonomy. Moral progress is dependent upon the emancipation of the rational individual from the heteronomous influences of tra-ditional morality.[7]

The premodern principle of right intention has largely been set aside as one of these questionable dispositions of traditional morality, or as irrelevant to morality (as are all intentions in consequentialist ethics), or has been redefined in terms of a rule (as in deontological ethics). As a result, right intention, understood as a disposition of character, is virtually absent in contemporary scholarship on *jus in bello.*[8]

The Impact of this Neglect

A rule-based approach to morality has made valuable contributions to better meeting moral demands, such as the codification of moral principles in international law.[9] Also, the reflection entailed by a rule-based approach is vital to a person's moral well-being, arguably demonstrated by the lack of reflection involved in some cases of moral injury among soldiers.[10] However, the rise of a rule-based framework at the exclusion of a character-based approach has resulted in three shortcomings. First, it fosters a hollow, "checklist" technique in mil-itary ethics.[11] A checklist of moral rules can never accommodate the unanticipated and fast-developing circumstances that soldiers face, nor provide the forward-looking intention that soldiers require to navigate those circumstances.[12] As Coates observes, the "ubiquity of the unforeseen or unforeseeable [in war] impedes reflection and strengthens the claims of traditional morality."[13] Soldiers require a disposition toward a just and lasting peace (which, undoubtedly, implies a complementary, reflective understanding of that peace) to properly fulfill their duties. Extrinsic restraint cannot effectively replace intrinsic restraint.[14]

Second, an exclusive focus on rules produces an overly bureaucratic mindset among soldiers. They come to resemble Alasdair MacIntyre's bureaucratic manager, who "treats ends as given, as outside his scope..."[15] Instead of an ends-oriented rationality, this manager applies a bureaucratic "rationality of matching means to ends economically and efficiently," considering the ends themselves to be "predetermined."[16] There is little emphasis in military doctrine, training, or professional education for a genuine understanding of what military operations are meant to promote. The emphasis is on rules that ought to be followed.[17] The division between *jus ad bellum* and *jus in bello* (war's ends and war's means) can further reinforce this bureaucratic rationality, since the *ad bellum* issues are ultimately the responsibility of political leaders. Add in the US military's deference to civilian authority (appropriate as it is), and the analytical division of moral categories can deepen to a disturbing compartmentalization that seemingly absolves soldiers of an obligation to understand the moral underpinnings of their service. Soldiers are commonly seen, by themselves as well as others, as virtually automatons instead of moral agents.

Third, a strictly rule-based moral framework is deficient because reasoning alone does not prompt action, but requires a corresponding affective commitment to principles or values that lead to right action. "Reflective morality puts its faith in the rule. It neglects the fundamental issue of will and motivation by assuming (wrongly) the self-motivating power of reason."[18] This fact is especially pertinent given the contrary affective reactions that persons experience in stressful situations like war. Traditional morality, with its focus on character traits instead of solely intellectual reflection, "acknowledges that, to be effective, moral judgements require the support of moral dispositions, feelings and inclinations."[19] It is, in this regard, more apt for the challenges of war. The principle of right intention emphasizes the *character* required for the pursuit of justice, not the *state of affairs* required to realize justice (as does the principle of just cause). Thus, right intention is an indispensable component of *jus in bello*.

A Worse Intention

The checklist, the bureaucratic mindset, and the myth of reason alone prompting action all set the conditions for a thoroughgoing disposition to develop among many soldiers (and, indirectly, many civilians) that their essential purpose is to kill – killing is their *raison d'etre*. The lethal act is not considered a regrettable, though necessary, task that is subordinate to the goal of a just and lasting peace. Instead, the act fills the void in military culture left by the absence of right intention as a guiding principle. It is a confusion of task and purpose. If there is no cultivation of a disposition toward a just peace, then there will be a disposition toward something else; a disposition-less soldier is an impossibility. In the worst case, a disposition forms toward killing for its own sake, involving a kind of dark-hearted relish for it. More often, and only marginally better, is a disposition toward a "negative peace," the kind established by eliminating the enemy.[20] This aim is what the ancient historian Tacitus had in mind when he noted "where [empires] make a desert, they call it peace."[21]

This negative peace may be legitimate in extreme cases of aggressors who are fanatically committed to the elimination of others. However, soldiers (and, again, civilians) should not be *disposed* to this peace, but only settle for it when these circumstances arise. Their disposition should remain toward a peace involving a reconciliatory coexistence within an international community, a harmony between political bodies based on justice, instead of toward an absence of conflict because only one political body remains standing. Even a softer version of this negative peace, in which adversaries are subjugated instead of outright killed, rarely meets the standards of justice and should, therefore, rarely be taken up as the peace to aim for. Besides being unjust, such a peace will rarely last: "The peace of subdued men is not genuine peace, but a peace marked by profound instability ...."[22]

When soldiers understand peace only negatively, they elevate killing too prominently. Killing is treated casually and more efficaciously than it really is, especially when professional norms promote an application of moral principles with the insufficient depth of a legalistic checklist, the mechanical efficiency of a bureaucracy, and the detached indifference of an automaton. A sobering example is the Vietnam War, with political and military leaders emphasizing quantifiable metrics of progress, chiefly the notorious body count.[23] More recently, in a presidential election debate of 2015, candidate Mike Huckabee commented, "The purpose of the military is to kill people and break things."[24] While possibly said more for rhetorical effect than plain truth, the sound bite still sparked a public discussion that reveals the disposition of many soldiers toward merely a negative peace and the killing entailed by it.[25]

Another example: Admiral Michael Mullen, as chairman of the Joint Chiefs of Staff in 2008, advised members of Congress that "We can't kill our way to victory" in Afghanistan.[26] Two retired military officers argued that Mullen was wrong, that soldiers needed to be free of the "timidity" behind Mullen's comment in order to "act with the necessary savagery and purposefulness to destroy...Islamic terrorists worldwide."[27] In the retired officers' review of military history to support their point, making a desert and calling it peace appears to be the only state of affairs to seek with military forces. It is noteworthy that these two officers served as military lawyers in Iraq and Afghanistan, advising field commanders on rules of engagement and obligations under international law (which, they state, should be bent in favor of one's own forces).[28]

A charitable reading of their argument requires distinguishing between two notions of victory. Presumably, Mullen refers to victory in the overall effort at establishing a stable Afghan regime that can resist the unrest of violent extremist groups and provide for its citizens, such that extremists find no safe haven or support. The two officers, however, are focused on tactical victory in combat. What is more, they seem to define victory at any scale in terms of tactical conflict. The stance of these officers reveals an underlying assumption that international relations, and the wars those relations sometimes generate, are always zero-sum games. While moments of actual combat qualify, it is important to never lose sight of the context outside of those violent clashes, where another's gain is not necessarily one's own loss (and vice versa), and where something better than a negative peace is possible. Where this better peace is an option, we are morally and prudentially obliged to pursue it. This obligation is what is meant by right intention. It is a disposition toward a positive peace, an insistence on keeping an eye on its possibility, even in the midst of concessions otherwise.[29]

A disposition toward a negative peace and its corresponding fixation on killing is easier to maintain if enemies are considered less than human. Subhuman adversaries (commonly animals or insects) arguably do not warrant the kind of restraint one grants to fellow humans, nor the same commitment to a shared future. Besides the social influences of nationalism, racism, or negative cultural stereotypes, the ostensible justice of one's war can prevent one from seeing the enemy "as anything other than a criminal, and as such subject to anything he has coming to him."[30] This crusading mentality can be one more pressure to dehumanize enemies, as well as the noncombatants associated with them. Instead of a subhuman status of an insect, however, the crusading mentality casts enemies as morally evil monsters.[31] Killing becomes a central moral obligation, whatever peace it produces.

In addition, a killing intention is easier to maintain with a militaristic view of war. If war is considered to have intrinsic value, a nobility with no recognition of its tragedy, then the killing it entails is not regretted, but embraced. This militaristic stance is often a coping mechanism for soldiers confronted with the tension between the *prima facie* immorality of killing and yet the apparent duty to kill. Instead of working through this tension (which might propel her to the principle of right intention), the soldier may dismiss the former and settle on the latter, usually with the help of others in a similar predicament and due to cultural forces at large. As one veteran describes it, "Once you learn to push past immoral behavior, it becomes easier."[32]

A killing intention, dehumanization, and militarism all reinforce each other in a military culture unanchored by a disposition to a just and lasting peace. An analogy with surgery can help illustrate the danger of distorting the soldier's overarching purpose.[33] No one wants to be the patient of a surgeon obsessed with surgery, ignoring what would actually contribute to full health. As much as the surgeon's skill with a scalpel matters, her essential purpose remains the promotion of physical well-being. She should not attempt surgery just because she has the authority and the skill to do it. She should fully understand when, and in what way, wielding her scalpel will best contribute to that health. She also must be able to adjust to unforeseen details or complications during the surgery. In the same way, soldiers must expertly wield lethal force, but must also understand the just peace that the killing act is supposed to promote, understand when lethal force may undermine it, and adjust their actions in unexpected circumstances to still bring it about. As the American general John Schofield noted in 1881, "the object and end in war is *not* 'to kill.' This is but one of the *means* necessary to that end …. The object of war is to conquer an honorable, advantageous, and lasting peace."[34] When soldiers have no appreciation of this peace nor a commitment to it, as entailed by the principle of right intention, they are dangerously ill-equipped to wield lethal force wisely.

Reviving Right Intention

So far, I have highlighted the neglect of right intention as a principle of *jus in bello*, the resulting void that enables a killing intention to grow in its place, and the dehumanization and militarism that stems from, and reinforces, a killing intention. Empathy helps to alleviate these moral – and, importantly, practical – concerns. In this section, I aim to show empathy's resistance to dehumanization and militarism, its role in undermining a killing intention, and its contribution to a right intention.

Empathy Reveals the Enemy's Moral Equivalence

In the previous chapter, I clarified the kind of solidarity that empathy entails: not a solidarity of opinions, perspectives, judgments, values, or feelings, but only a solidarity of fundamental personhood. It may contribute to the former, but not necessarily so. Empathy, as an experiential understanding of another person, reveals the humanity that a soldier has in common with his enemy. Empathy humanizes others and, therefore, counters dehumanizing tendencies. Lower-level empathy grounds an intuition of the enemy's human status, something akin to sense perception. This lower-level empathy can be attenuated or interrupted, like closing one's eyes to interrupt sight, but without such action, lower-level empathy occurs automatically. Higher-level empathy builds on this intuition through cognitive processes like imaginative perspective-taking to reveal insights about the other's experience, including elements of its narrative structure, worldview, values, and intentions. Higher-level empathy is not automatic, but must be consciously initiated. It is, however, normally habituated.

As an example, consider my soldier's experience that I summarized at the end of the first chapter. Through military training and enculturation, he interrupted his lower-level empathy for the sake of forceful actions in raiding the Iraqi colonel's house. After the forced entry, the shooting of a person reasonably deemed threatening, and the securing of the rest of the house, the soldiers attempted to stabilize the wounded colonel. In the shift from forceful actions to assessing the immediate situation and treating the colonel, the intuition of lower-level empathy returned, particularly to my one soldier, as something received instead of suppressed. His higher-level empathy processed the intuition and expanded on it to foster an understanding of the colonel as a husband and a father. In turn, this realization spurred the soldier's empathetic understanding of the widow and daughter. In this experiential understanding, this moment of empathy, my soldier also became troubled.

The source of his disturbance was at least partly due to the deceased Iraqi's more complicated status. He was no longer purely or simply an enemy combatant to be fought, but was also a dead human being to be mourned. My soldier paused over the fact that he and this colonel were both husbands and they were both fathers of little girls. It had been easier to peremptorily consider the colonel a criminal who was personally responsible for this war in which my soldier found himself. The corresponding hatred for the guilty enemy made it easier to kick in the door and pull the trigger. Now, however, this hatred had been...

> interrupted or overridden by a more reflective understanding...
> the sense that the enemy soldier, though his war may be criminal,
> is nevertheless as blameless as oneself. Armed, he is an enemy;
> but he isn't *my* enemy in any specific sense; the war itself isn't a
> relation between persons but between political entities and their
> human instruments .... [Like me, they find themselves] trapped in
> a war they didn't make. I find in them my moral equals.[35]

My soldier's empathetic experience maps well onto Michael Walzer's claim of the moral equality of combatants. Empathy revealed that this colonel was an instrument of a political entity, just as my soldier was. The colonel was subject to social influences, various authorities, pressures, and desires that coalesced to bring him into the conflict; again, just as my soldier was. Continuing this higher-level empathy, my soldier might ask himself,

> What would it take for me to cooperate with a foreign occupying force patrolling my hometown? What behavior on their part would truly win my cooperation? How likely might I be to take up arms against the foreign occupying force?

These questions risk the error of projection since they prompt self-oriented perspective-taking, which incorporates many influences that differ from the colonel's. However, self-oriented perspective-taking can be an appropriate mode of higher-level empathy "when there is a great deal of overlap between self and other or where the situation is the type that would lead to a fairly universal response."[36] It seems plausible that foreign soldiers patrolling the streets of one's neighborhood prompts a similar concern for the safety of one's family, perhaps a similar patriotism, and a similar distrust of strangers from a foreign culture.

Walzer goes on to define moral equality quite strongly, making it a necessary consequence of combatant status that they are blameless for the war itself.[37] On the one hand, an empathetic understanding of a combatant seems to underscore this moral equality. Empathy highlights the fog of loyalties, international complexities, perceived danger, and propaganda within which soldiers on both sides would have to judge the morality of their countries' war. It is unfair to insist that soldiers see past that fog.

On the other hand, a genuine application of empathy will highlight the grievances of the other side, improving the chances that a soldier (and any fellow citizen) can weigh competing claims and more accurately judge the morality of the war's impetus. Further, an empathetic soldier better grasps how she, her unit, and her country are perceived and experienced in the course of the war. Empathy can sometimes penetrate the fog, at least to some extent. In this manner, empathy promotes objectivity in judgment (as suggested at the end of Chapter 2), inoculating the soldier from naïvely thinking that her country's position is infallibly correct. (I acknowledge that empathy with one's in-group, especially one's country, often endorses such infallibility; that is one danger of selective empathy.) Such judgment is a necessary component of citizenship in a democracy – and soldiers remain citizens.[38]

Walzer's moral equality of combatants attempts to exonerate all soldiers of any responsibility for *jus ad bellum* judgments; however, empathetic knowledge resists this wholesale assumption. It helps identify who warrants such exoneration and who does not. It sheds light on the particular influences, authorities, limitations, and freedoms a combatant may have. In doing so, empathy may actually heighten condemnation of a combatant's choices because it reveals genuine alternatives, some of which may be morally obligatory. Empathy, therefore, undermines the moral equality of combatants as conceived in Walzer's legalist paradigm. Instead, it points to the just war tradition's earlier voices who did not separate *jus ad bellum* and *jus in bello* so stringently.

At the same time, empathy does not wholly reinforce the contrary stance that soldiers simply are responsible for the wars they fight. An empathetic understanding includes a grasp of all the forces acting on the soldier, especially during the ramp-up to war. Soldiers are commonly excused for their war's violation of *jus ad bellum*. The real point of contention is how broad and automatic this excusal should be. All I want to point out is that empathetically considering a soldier reveals the variety of factors affecting their moral agency. Empathy provides a granularity that refines our judgment about a soldier's situation and corresponding responsibility. By empathetically putting ourselves "in the soldier's shoes," we can ascertain how much excuse to grant – if any.

While empathy does not endorse the moral equality of combatants, it does underscore their equivalent moral nature, consisting of moral value, moral agency (that is subject to various influences and limits), and moral responsibility (adjusted in light of those influences and limits). In helping soldiers recognize the moral equivalence of enemies, empathy provides a "check on a wartime inclination" to dehumanize.[39] It undermines the tendency to see enemies as lesser animals or as so evil that their humanity falls away. They are, instead, perceived as being subject to similar influences of nationalistic fervor, respect for laws of conscription, and a desire to protect their families and fellow countrymen. This honesty regarding one's enemies can have two effects. First, it instills greater restraint, such that soldiers more reliably keep acts of force to only those that are genuinely necessary. Second, it lays the groundwork for a disposition toward a just and lasting peace shared with former adversaries, instead of a negative peace secured by their elimination or subjugation.

Empathy's Relation to Killing

"To our modern mind," Shay observes, "the enemy is detestable – by definition."[40] Maintaining the humanity of the enemy is commonly considered impossible; for many it is a self-evident truth "that men cannot kill an enemy understood to be honorable and like oneself."[41] Contrary to the argument that soldiers must dehumanize enemies to kill them, however, there are at least some moments when they cannot dehumanize enemies because of intimate encounters with them. Walzer offers some of these instances, drawing on veterans' memoirs in which they describe the difficulty of firing their weapons at enemy soldiers "who look funny, who are taking a bath, holding up their pants [as they run along a trench], reveling in the sun, [or] smoking a cigarette."[42] Richard Holmes observes that the "concept of a hateful and inhuman enemy rarely survives contact with him as an individual."[43] My troubled soldier's experience above also illustrates the unavoidable empathetic moments of war. These moments are, admittedly, only brief glimpses at the humanity of individuals, glimpses that are often buried under the propaganda of the war effort and the piercing emotions of struggle and loss inherent to war. However, simply stifling these empathetic moments leads to the dangers of dehumanization, militarism, and killing as one's overarching purpose. Right intention is lost. (It also leads to the danger of moral injury, which I will take up in the next chapter.) In reconciling the humanity of enemies with the duty to kill them, there must be an alternative to dehumanization, which merely tries to deny the former.[44]

Michael Brough asks this same question: "How, then, should soldiers view the killings they commit in war, and how should nations teach their soldiers to view them? Dehumanization is too costly."[45] Drawing on the research of psychologists David Grossman and Stanley Milgram, Brough concedes a necessity to distance oneself from one's target in order to kill him. This distance may take a physical form, especially as enabled by modern technologies, but it may also take an emotional form, including "social distance (which emphasizes differences in social caste), cultural distance (which accentuates racial and ethnic differences), and moral distance (which envisions the enemy's moral inferiority)."[46] These latter forms of emotional distance are precisely the dehumanizing tendencies that make enemies either "base, as an animal or insect, or evil, as a monster or demon," and are, therefore, unacceptable.[47] Brough labels these attempts at distance "subhumanization" to denote their denial of an enemy's human worth. In their place, he suggests an alternative form of emotional distance that he calls "nonhumanization." Prompted by the physical distance of modern weaponry, "nonhumanization began with the invention of indirect trajectory artillery, when enemy soldiers became pushpins or pencil dots on maps, or shouted coordinates to a gun section."[48] Perceiving the enemy as nonhuman "blips on a computer screen" has expanded as warfare has increasingly become electronically mediated.[49]

Instead of an emotionally charged belittling of the enemy, nonhumanization involves an emotionless objectifying of the enemy. It may, therefore, be a few moral degrees better than subhumanization, given the violent excesses that the latter invites. However, even though the *non* prefix avoids the connotation of lesser value that *sub* does, it still conveys the sense that the enemy is *un*-human, something other than human. Thus, it still seems a problematic approach to the justified killing of other *humans* in war. Brough is quick to point out this concern, saying that considering enemies nonhuman can deny their moral equivalence in a similar way to considering enemies subhuman.[50] Given the need for some kind of emotional distance, however, or some way of "making killing easier" in the right moral circumstances, Brough endorses a nonhumanizing moment, though one tightly bounded by a respect for the enemy.[51] The killing of another, he suggests, "does not preclude honoring the dead after the battle. A prayer, a thought, a muttered farewell might suffice as a sign of respect for the fallen." He highlights the therapeutic research that shows how important it is for soldiers to honor fallen adversaries in order to avert "damaging psychological repercussions."[52]

I am sympathetic to Brough's effort, but I want to offer a subtle alternative to nonhumanization. The soldier who finds herself in circumstances such that killing the enemy is at least morally permissible, and possibly obligatory, should keep the humanity of the enemy intact, but detach herself from her empathetic impulse that underscores that humanity. I already suggested this alternative above when I traced the roles of lower-level and higher-level empathy in the experience of my troubled soldier. This alternative is similar to the surgeon's need to emotionally detach from the patient to best perform a surgery. Just as the surgeon should not be expected to empathetically perceive or imagine the experience he is causing in the patient, at least in the midst of the surgical act, so the soldier should not be expected to empathetically engage with her enemy during the lethal act. Also just like the surgeon, however, the soldier should not maintain the detachment afterward (and often cannot, as demonstrated most starkly by morally injured soldiers). The parallel exists in the responsibilities of senior soldiers, as well:

> it is a necessary part of high military command in the field that a commander should callous himself against the human cost of his plans and orders – otherwise it would be emotionally impossible for him to do his job. This need not make him deficient in care before battle or in compassion after it, however. It need not make him inhumane...[53]

It is possible that I am splitting hairs in trying to distinguish between Brough's nonhumanization and my interruption of one's empathetic impulse. However, it does seem relevant to describe the necessary step not as an actual attribution of nonhuman status to the enemy, but instead as a management of one's own faculties. Over time, a disposition will develop based on one or the other. It seems better to limit that disposition to how one emotionally responds to others rather than forming a habit of objectifying others. The more limited disposition will better enable a soldier to respect deceased enemies in the manner Brough recommends, since their humanity is never set aside. Nonhumanization too easily lends itself to the dangers of a bureaucratic mindset or a checklist approach to *jus in bello*, putting the maintenance of a right intention at risk.

So instead of dehumanizing enemies as either subhuman or nonhuman, I suggest a management of one's empathy that is similar to the management of one's senses. Just as one can attune one's ear to detect certain sounds over others, one can focus one's empathy in selective ways. This empathetic attunement already happens in various contexts, and there are immoral moments of it in which we get too selective. This partiality is particularly common in war, where the empathy with one's comrades can drown out the empathy with enemies or noncombatants. The case of justified killing in war, however, counts as a morally appropriate moment.

Shannon French and Anthony Jack offer important neuroscientific insights that inform this management of one's empathetic impulse. They cite research showing that "the tension between analytic and empathetic thinking is an inescapable feature of our evolutionary heritage" and "...we cannot be both analytic and empathetic at the same time." They further point out that the soldier's challenging circumstances require her "to be both highly analytic and highly empathetic." However, there is a "natural cycling between analytic and empathetic mental modes" that, as long as it is managed well, is "likely to be more healthy and sustainable, and less fatiguing, than a work environment that only calls on one of these cognitive modes."[54] While French and Jack conclude a "mechanistic dehumanization" (equivalent to Brough's nonhumanization) is necessary, I remain concerned with the growth of a morally problematic disposition in the soldier, as noted above.

Outside of this concession for the justified killing act (and, relatedly, other justified acts of lesser force), empathy should not be suppressed in war. Indeed, it cannot be, at least with any finality, given the instinctive nature of lower-level empathy, the unavoidable empathetic moments that occur even in war, and the introspection that follows combat for most every soldier. Soldiers are humans, and therefore, are hard-wired for empathy, making the human automaton an impossible goal, even with extensive military training. It is also an immoral goal, since an automaton cannot maintain a disposition to a just and lasting peace, but must be equipped with merely a program of activity, and therefore lacks the judgment needed to properly wield lethal force across the range of circumstances a soldier may face. Third, it is a tactically foolish goal: an automaton cannot adapt to genuinely novel circumstances since it is only equipped with a checklist, however elaborate.

What Else Besides Dehumanizing?

Given the unavoidable nature of empathy, and the humanization of others that empathy prompts, and the vital moral need to keep others humanized in war, it is important to identify alternatives to the modern view that leaves no room for the humanity of the enemy. This modern view suggests that a soldier's valor depends upon, and is even proven by, a disdainful or dismissive degradation of the enemy. Consider, instead, the attitude of the ancient Greeks as portrayed by Homer, or, most tellingly, the attitude of early Christians, which allow for an enemy to be understood as "honorable like oneself" even when fighting to the death.[55]

In Jonathan Shay's extensive study of Homer's *Iliad*, he found no instance of Greeks or Trojans dehumanizing each other in their battle over Troy.[56] Neither side referred to the other with derogatory terms, which is a common practice in modern wars, nor did they express disrespect, more generally. On the contrary, the two sides repeatedly expressed admiration for the fighting prowess of their adversaries. After an extended duel that ends in a draw, the Trojan warrior Ajax states:

> We'll meet again another time – and fight until the unseen power decides between those hosts of ours, awarding one or the other victory. Afterwards they'll say, among [Greeks] and Trojans: "These two fought and gave no quarter in close combat, yet they parted as friends."[57]

Shay notes that the "contrast to fighting 'Gooks' in Vietnam cannot be sharper."[58]

The important exception to this respectful attitude is the appalling treatment of Hektor's body after Achilles defeats him in battle. Achilles mutilates the corpse and shamefully drags it on a public display. As Shay points out, though, this behavior was condemned by Greeks and Trojans alike, violating deep-seated norms that they shared.[59] What is more, Homer portrays Achilles as especially respectful and generous toward adversaries prior to his change of character early in the story, which was spurred by his commanding officer's betrayal.

Admittedly, the Greeks and Trojans shared a common culture that made respect easier to maintain. It was not as difficult for one side to view the other as equal in human status and corresponding value. Shay notes that "later Greeks did debase foreign, 'barbarian' enemies every bit as much as modern Americans [did in World War II and Vietnam]."[60] Nonetheless, the Greek and Trojan example stands as an important exception to the presumed need for dehumanization to fulfill soldierly duties. As respectably as the Greeks and Trojans perceived each other, it did not dilute their fighting tenacity.[61]

Shay attributes the contrast between the ancient Greek attitude toward enemies and its modern counterpart to an inherent tendency to dehumanize adversaries in Abrahamic religions.[62] The Jewish, Christian, and Islamic traditions, in Shay's view, emphasize the dehumanization of enemies as an expression of piety. "When modern American soldiers and their leaders dehumanize the enemy, they affirm their loyalty to God, expressing a cultural tradition powerfully engraved by biblical scripture."[63] Shay examines the story of David and Goliath, highlighting speech that compares Goliath to animals and presents him "as a moral monstrosity as well as a physical monster, not conceivable as a counterpart in political settlement...."[64] Shay concludes:

> The Judeo-Christian (and Islamic) world view has triumphed so completely over the Homeric world view that dishonoring the enemy now seems natural, virtuous, patriotic, pious. Yet in the *Iliad* only Achilles disrespects the enemy. In Homer's world, this is not a natural but an inhuman state into which Achilles has tragically fallen. Homer's warriors are never weakened by respecting the enemy.[65]

There is no denying the dehumanization that has been done in the name of God, nor the religious fervor that too often fuels it. Yet, Shay's contention seems lopsided and incomplete. In his analysis of David's comments about and to Goliath, it is not as clear as Shay claims that David reduces Goliath to the lesser status of an animal or monster. David compares the challenge of fighting him to his prior challenges of fighting a lion and a bear, but this comparison is not necessarily demeaning; it may also be read as a recognition of Goliath's ferocity. David clearly draws courage from his belief of having God's favor, and this presumption can lead to an arrogant and contemptuous view of others, but it is not apparent that David is displaying arrogance or contempt. It could be confidence and a desire to give God the credit for the victory that he anticipates.

Regardless, the bigger concern is Shay's silence on the Jewish, Christian, and Islamic traditions' scriptural advocacy for humane treatment of enemies and outsiders. I will focus on the Christian tradition, both because its early members were foundational to the just war tradition and because the Christian mandate regarding enemies is so drastic: as Jesus famously declared, they are to be loved.[66]

Many find this injunction untenable; it is a contradiction for a soldier to claim that she loves the enemy whom she kills. Perhaps the

this doctrine is differentiating between what soldiers *intend* and what soldiers *foresee*.[77] As Walzer stipulates, "The intention of the [soldier] is good, that is, he aims only at the acceptable effect; the evil effect is not one of his ends, nor is it a means to his ends."

Walzer adds an important amendment to the doctrine of double effect: "Double effect is defensible, I want to argue, only when the two outcomes are the product of a *double intention*: first, that the 'good' be achieved; second, that the foreseeable evil be reduced as far as possible."[78] Soldiers must intend only the acceptable effect, and must actively intend to minimize the unacceptable effect, "accepting costs to himself."[79] Walzer acknowledges a limit to these costs, but emphasizes that soldiers have a duty to take on more risk than noncombatants. It is part of the essence of soldiering. He settles on the admittedly vague limit that soldiers must exercise "due care" toward noncombatants.[80]

Empathy improves soldiers' judgments about this due care because it keeps noncombatants as humans instead of anything less. One example is Klay's account above of the Marines caring for the wounded insurgent. David Wood provides another example of this due care in practice. A former Special Forces officer recounted the actions of a comrade during a firefight:

> "We were exchanging gunfire from, I mean, like here to there," he said, gesturing at the ten-foot distance from my dining room table into the kitchen. "Two women were shot. Who shot them? I don't know. But in this gunfire between these al-Qaeda guys and us, these women and a child ran between us, and [a Special Forces trooper named] Scott Gross, about six-three, two hundred forty pounds, put his weapon system down as gunfire is exchanging, picked up the small child, turned his back to the gunfire, crashed in this door, put the baby on the floor, turned around, and came back out..."[81]

Just as empathy helps soldiers maintain enemy combatants as humans, an empathetic understanding of noncombatants helps soldiers to maintain their humanity in decisions. When soldiers face the dilemma of harm to both combatants and noncombatants, empathy helps to foster Walzer's double intention, so that not only are combatants the sole intended target, but the risk to noncombatants is intentionally reduced. Thus, empathy improves the fulfillment of the principle of discrimination.

Proportionality

An empathetic understanding of enemies and noncombatants also has something to contribute to the *jus in bello* principle of proportionality. Under discrimination above, a notion of proportionality already appeared regarding the weighing of the acceptable effect of harming combatants against the unacceptable effect of harming noncombatants. Here, however, the focus is a different application of proportional calculation, a more general one that does not necessarily entail the dilemma above. The principle of proportionality is utilitarian, advocating the weighing of costs and benefits when deciding on military operations. The harm done (to combatants, even if no noncombatants are affected; and to land, resources, and infrastructure) must not outweigh the good achieved.

Like discrimination, proportionality is simple in concept and often complex in application. Apart from clear cases of extreme war crimes, judging what counts as excessive harm can be difficult. An empathetic understanding of those involved – enemies, allies, neutral parties – helps to more accurately judge. This judgment requires more than a basic factual understanding of the consequences: who and how many might die, what property will be destroyed, what land will be secured, what opportunities will be made available, etc. It also requires an empathetic understanding of those consequences. What value or meaning is placed on the consequences by the relevant actors? How will the consequences be differently interpreted by those affected? How will the consequences impact others' attitudes toward ending the conflict? In considering alternative perspectives on the proportionality of the military operation in question, soldiers can better anticipate the reactions of the enemy, of allies, and of noncombatants. This empathetic understanding can help soldiers recognize when their actions might be considered disproportionate, or "unnecessary, brutal, or unfair" by others.[82] This opinion of others is not authoritative, but it remains relevant toward pursuing opportunities for peace. Empathy thus refines soldiers' judgments on what is proportionate in military operations.

Empathy in War-Waging

The preceding consideration of empathy's role in fulfilling the principles of discrimination and proportionality falls under James Dubik's war-fighting portion of *jus in bello*. Empathy also has an important role in the activities of his other portion of *jus in bello*, war-waging. In this section, I will examine empathy's contribution to strategic planning and assessing progress. As Dubik notes,

> While final decision authority rests on a very small group –
> sometimes a single individual – decisions of this magnitude are
> preceded by detailed analysis of alternatives, feasibility studies,
> and reams of paper reflecting the arguments that had been con-
> ducted by numerous committees and study groups as well as sub-
> ordinate organizations and staff agencies. The quality of the final
> decisions often reflected the quality of the preparatory work.[83]

My claim is that empathy improves the preparatory work and the final decision, but as a veteran of numerous committees, study groups,
and staff sections, I recognize that these roles, and the windowless
offices that often accompany them, can stifle empathetic consideration
of others (in some ways, more completely than the vagaries of combat).
Yet the consequences at stake demand the best in comprehending the
worldview and motivations of human actors, in thinking critically and
creatively, in rigorously scrutinizing one's assumptions, and assessing
progress honestly and meaningfully. Furthermore, in doing this work
well, one helps to maintain the legitimacy of the war, at least in one
respect. Legitimacy, Dubik points out, is a

> function of the righteousness of the war (a *jus ad bellum* issue) and
> progress toward probable success (a *jus in bello* issue). [It] is tied
> directly to the competence of senior political and military leaders
> in executing their war-waging responsibilities.[84]

As empathy improves the planning and assessment process, it also
helps to secure genuine progress, thus contributing to legitimacy.

War-waging activities are more reflective than war-fighting, and
therefore involve a more reflective approach to the moral issues at
hand. This facet of war-waging prompts an addendum to Coates' critique of a strictly rule-based, reflective approach to military ethics.
While he argues in favor of a character-based approach, it is the exclusive grounding of morality in rules by some proponents that fuels
Coates' concern. Both matter, as Coates would seem to agree.[85] The
way they matter differs, though, between war-fighting and war-waging. War-fighting leans more on instinctual character traits and less on
reflection, due to the urgency of decisions and the visceral experience
of combat. War-waging decisions are often less urgent and visceral, but
weightier and more complex, and therefore, warrant greater reflection.

The realm of war-waging requires a default stance of "don't just do something – stand there," instead of the normal stance of war-fighting, "don't just stand there – do something."[86]

Similarly, the reflective nature of war-waging activities lends themselves to higher-level empathy. Lower-level empathy remains relevant, but war-waging can be complemented more fully with its more cognitive counterpart. This change in the type of empathy employed rests on the change in the type of challenges between war-fighting and war-waging.

Strategic Planning

In Dubik's analysis of the kinds of problems soldiers face in war, he distinguishes between technical problems and adaptive problems.[87] Technical problems are those that soldiers can remedy with their current knowledge and experience; the problems "can be resolved through the application of authoritative expertise and the organization's current structures, procedures, and ways of doing things."[88] Technical problems may be complicated, but their solution is readily discernable. Adaptive problems, on the other hand, fall outside an organization's normal capacities and are usually hard to understand, let alone solve. The context of an adaptive problem is "continually changing," and therefore "the solution changes continually as well."[89] Dubik observes that the tactical challenges in war are generally technical in nature, while the strategic challenges are usually adaptive. Thus, war-waging involves mostly adaptive problems.

The first, and most important, step in handling adaptive problems is grasping them properly. One of the most basic challenges to this step is recognizing the shortcomings of one's own conceptual frameworks. When an adaptive problem involves human actors, especially enemies, empathetically understanding those humans helps to overcome the faults of pre-existing conceptions of them. In other words, empathy helps to overcome cultural, ideological, racial, or social biases and prejudices. For example, an empathetic approach toward the Japanese in World War II would have humanized them and made it harder to underestimate their capabilities. Instead, racist stereotypes had convinced Allied planners early in the war that the Japanese were "too nearsighted and prone to vertigo to fly a combat aircraft; too fearful to fight in jungles, which they supposedly believed were inhabited by ghosts and demons."[90] Underestimating enemies leads to needless loss of lives.

When facing adaptive problems, there can be an overriding temptation to define the problem as a technical one, instead. Especially in

military culture with its emphasis on action, the enticing option is to
treat an unfamiliar, inconvenient problem with a familiar and conven-
ient solution. As an example of this error, consider the rise and fall of
a military planning construct called "Effects-Based Operations," or
EBO.[91]

EBO was a planning construct originating with the US Air Force,
but employed in one form or another by the other services, as well.[92]
It derives its name from a strict focus on the damaging effects to be
achieved against enemy forces rather than a more generic focus on
the amount of resources to apply against the enemy (in terms of units,
ammunition, or weapon systems). Air Force planners developed EBO
to more efficiently employ resources against key nodes of an enemy's
forces. For example, a pilot might target a radar system that provides
crucial data to several enemy air defense weapon systems, rather than
target each of the air defense systems themselves. Besides using fewer
resources, this approach paralyzed the enemy with more selective, simultaneous attacks. EBO saw its first major application in the success-
ful air campaign of 1990 as the initial part of the campaign to drive
Saddam's forces out of Kuwait. The construct of EBO also produced
the "shock and awe" air campaign at the outset of the 2003 invasion
of Iraq.

The procedures of EBO guided military planners in accounting for
all relevant factors of an enemy force's capabilities. In this way, it was
an effort in "mapping all knowledge onto a manipulable grid."[93] When
analyzing a relatively closed system, such as the air defense weapons
above, EBO proved useful in highlighting the enemy's vulnerabilities
and steering the judicious application of military force. However, the
tactical successes resulting from EBO planning prompted the exten-
sion of EBO to larger strategic concerns. Planners attempted to cap-
ture political, military, economic, and social factors in a much more
ambitious manipulable grid, coming to treat "something as complex
as human activity [as] an essentially passive and lifeless domain."[94] In
the place of air defense radars, for example, tribal leaders became the
key nodes to be "targeted" with available resources. EBO thinking
drew attention away from traditional considerations of superior combat power or maintaining a reserve force in the case of surprises, and
instead promised, with a tantalizing level of certainty and efficiency, a
dismantled enemy stymied into submission. By 2008, critiques of this
planning construct began to emerge:

> Concepts with such labels as network-centric warfare, rapid de-
> cisive operations, shock and awe, and various permutations of

effects-based operations embraced what increasingly appeared as a faith-based argument that future war would lie mainly in the realm of certainty and therefore could be won quickly and efficiently, at low cost by small forces.[95]

Later that same year, a senior military commander in charge of doctrine issued a disparaging memorandum that banned US forces from using EBO for military planning.[96] The commander noted that EBO "mechanistically attempts to provide certainty and predictability in an inherently uncertain environment," is "too prescriptive and over-engineered," and "discounts the human dimensions of war (e.g., passion, imagination, willpower and unpredictability)."[97] He agreed that

> Elements of [EBO] have proven useful in addressing 'closed systems,' such as targeting where effects can be measured per USAF's deliberate analysis and targeting methods. However, the concepts have been misapplied by others to operations beyond their original intent, resulting in overextension and confusion.[98]

The title of this planning construct, *Effects-Based* Operations, implies greater wisdom than this critique has allowed. Indeed, focusing on desired effects truly can make the selection of means both more efficient and more ethically respectable (minimizing collateral damage, for example). However, the application of EBO to larger strategic concerns rested on a hubristic assumption that the military force could actually manipulate certain effects into existence with no need to accommodate unpredictable behavior of the enemy or others, nor a need to garner the cooperation of allies and key groups of noncombatants. This error was, metaphorically, an attempt to *manufacture* effects that could only be *farmed* – military units could not control all the factors (specifically, uncooperative humans) but vainly assumed otherwise. It is an epistemological error, in that soldiers failed to acknowledge the limits of what they could actually control. The planning construct promised too much certainty in achieving desired effects. The mistake was in attempting to turn a tactical planning construct that was suitable against closed systems of material components into a strategic planning construct for open, unpredictable systems with human components. A greater appreciation for empathy, for the understanding that it provides and the respect that it entails, would have prevented the assumption that the desired effects could be manufactured.

Besides the epistemological error in treating an adaptive problem as a technical one, the EBO planning construct involved a moral error in treating humans as things amenable to law-like generalizations. This moral error is a form of dehumanization; it objectifies human actors in a manner akin to Brough's nonhumanization above. In this mode, military planners employ cultural knowledge inappropriately, treating the knowledge as laws of behavior akin to the laws of physics. Planners approach enemies or others in a mechanical fashion and cast simplistic assumptions across whole populations. It is often a bureaucratic dehumanization, not necessarily a visceral subhumanization like in the stress of combat, though it may also stem from the latter. Regardless, it has effects just as troubling morally and practically. This kind of dehumanizing leads to treating war as a physical science and human actors as merely manipulable objects. So, "Effects-Based Operations" is a misleading title because the effects were chosen peremptorily from a moment of, at the least, bureaucratic dehumanization. As proposed in the last chapter, empathy is an antidote for this dehumanizing predisposition toward war as a physical science and toward cultural knowledge as merely law-like generalizations of others.

Assessment

Empathy improves the assessment of progress by keeping the focus of assessment on outputs instead of merely inputs. In dealing with the confusion of the counterinsurgencies in Iraq and Afghanistan, US personnel faced a constant temptation to assess their progress based exclusively on inputs, which are easier to control. Nonetheless, one State Department leader of a provincial reconstruction team in Iraq reflected,

> We measured the impact of our projects by their effect on us, not by their effect on the Iraqis. *Output* was the word missing from the vocabulary of developing Iraq. Everything was measured only by what we put in – dollars spent, hours committed, people engaged…press releases written.[99]

Empathy's nature as a receptive mode toward another's experience steers soldiers from a focus on input to output and incorporates the population's view of military efforts. While the judgments of local citizens should not serve as the sole factor in the assessment of progress, their judgments should comprise one piece of that assessment, especially given the cooperative rebuilding efforts inherent to counterinsurgencies (or in the aftermath of conventional conflicts).

Another reason inputs can dominate assessments is their easy measurement. With the ever-present pressure of time, military planners can easily succumb to this error. Empathy, however, reduces this temptation toward easy measurement because it emphasizes a more holistic assessment of military operations that includes the opinions of allies, neutral parties, and noncombatants. Again, these empathetic understandings should not be the sole consideration in assessing progress, but they remain important, nonetheless.

If caught in a bureaucratic, overly quantitative mindset, planners and leaders fail to assess the war effort accurately. Recall the example of the Vietnam War, in which this kind of mindset combined with a killing intention to produce quantitative metrics such as body count to measure progress. One military historian remarked that, when stuck in this mindset, "If you can't count what's important, what you can count becomes important."[100] Empathy, with its humanization of others, and its spur toward a right intention, helps to offset this error by shifting the focus to a just and lasting peace between warring parties.

As in war-fighting above, a selective empathy can skew the assessment of progress instead of helping it. If leaders attend only to an empathetic understanding of soldiers, at the expense of a similar understanding of others, then the sole assessment criterion can become the safe return of every soldier, regardless of any progress in the mission at hand. This selective empathy can promote an overly risk-averse approach to military operations.

Conclusion

When the nature of soldiering is properly understood as oriented toward establishing a just and lasting peace, the role of empathy becomes clear and crucial. Empathy prompts soldiers to keep this peace as their intention, rather than seeking a negative peace that entails the subjugation or eradication of all adversaries. Empathy helps soldiers fend off the seemingly "universal wartime tradition" of dehumanizing enemy combatants and the civilians associated with them.[101] Instead, soldiers exercise appropriate restraint regarding forceful actions and improved judgment on when they are genuinely necessary. In this manner, soldiers better fulfill the war-fighting principles of discrimination and proportionality. This same empathetic understanding of others and corresponding right intention also improves soldiers' fulfillment of war-waging responsibilities in planning military campaigns within moral and practical constraints and assessing progress honestly and holistically.

Works Cited

Aquinas, Thomas (1485). *Summa theologiae*. Trans. Fathers of the English Dominican Province. Second and Revised Edition (1920). Online Edition Copyright © 2008 by Kevin Knight. <http://www.newadvent.org/summa/>.

Augustine (426 CE). *The City of God*. Trans. R. Ryson. Cambridge: Cambridge University Press (1998).

Augustine (c. 400 CE). *Contra Faustum* XXII, Trans. Richard Stothert. From *Nicene and Post-Nicene Fathers*, First Series, Vol. 4. Ed. Philip Schaff. Buffalo, NY: Christian Literature Publishing Co. (1887). Revised and edited for New Advent by Kevin Knight. <http://www.newadvent.org/fathers/140622.htm>.

Augustine. Letter 138 (c. 412 CE). Trans. J.G. Cunningham. From *Nicene and Post-Nicene Fathers*, First Series, Vol. 1. Ed. Philip Schaff. Buffalo, NY: Christian Literature Publishing Co. (1887). Revised and edited for New Advent by Kevin Knight. <http://www.newadvent.org/fathers/1102138.htm>.

Augustine. Letter 189 (c. 418 CE). Trans. J.G. Cunningham. From *Nicene and Post-Nicene Fathers*, First Series, Vol. 1. Ed. Philip Schaff. Buffalo, NY: Christian Literature Publishing Co. (1887). Revised and edited for New Advent by Kevin Knight. <http://www.newadvent.org/fathers/1102189.htm>.

Bell, Daniel (2009). *Just War as Christian Discipleship: Recentering the Tradition in the Church Rather Than the State*. Grand Rapids, MI: Brazos Press.

Biggar, Nigel (2013). *In Defence of War*. Oxford: Oxford University Press.

Bolgiano, David and John Taylor (2017). "Can't Kill Enough to Win? Think Again." *Proceedings Magazine*, Vol. 143/12/1,378. US Naval Institute (December 2017). <https:// www.usni.org/magazines/proceedings/2017-12/cant-kill-enough-win-think-again>.

Brough, Michael (2007). "Dehumanization of the Enemy and the Moral Equality of Soldiers." *Rethinking the Just War Tradition*. Eds. Michael Brough, John Lango, Harry van der Linden. Albany: SUNY Press, 149–167.

Burkhardt, Todd (2017). *Just War and Human Rights: Fighting with Right Intention*. Albany: SUNY Press.

Burns, Ken and Lynne Novick (2017). "The Vietnam War." Documentary. Florentine Films and WETA.

CNN Politics. "Troops Alone Will Not Yield Victory in Afghanistan." CNN.com (10 September 2008). <http://www.cnn.com/2008/POLITICS/09/10/mullen.afghanistan>.

Capizzi, Joseph (2015). *Politics, Justice, and War: Christian Governance and the Ethics of Warfare*. Oxford: Oxford University Press.

Cavanaugh, Matt (2015). "The Military's Purpose Is Not to Kill People and Break Things." *War on the Rocks* (26 August 2015). <https://warontherocks.com/2015/08/the-militarys-purpose-is-not-to-kill-people-and-break-things/>.

Cheek, Gary (2002). "Effects-Based Operations: The End of Dominant Maneuver?" *Transformation Concepts for National Security in the 21st Century*. Ed. Williamson Murray. Strategic Studies Institute, US Army War College, 73–100. <https://ssi.armywarcollege.edu/pubs/display.cfm?pubID=252>.

Coates, A.J. (2016). *The Ethics of War.* 2nd ed. Manchester: Manchester University Press.

Coplan, Amy (2011). "Understanding Empathy: Its Features and Effects." *Empathy: Philosophical and Psychological Perspectives.* Eds. Amy Coplan and Peter Goldie. New York: Oxford University Press, 3–18.

Dubik, James (2016). *Just War Reconsidered – Strategy, Ethics, and Theory.* Lexington: University Press of Kentucky.

French, Shannon (2017). *The Code of the Warrior: Exploring Warrior Values Past and Present.* 2nd ed. Lanham, MD: Rowman and Littlefield.

French, Shannon and Anthony Jack (2015). "Dehumanizing the Enemy: The Intersection of Neuroethics and Military Ethics." *Responsibilities to Protect: Perspectives in Theory and Practice.* Eds. David Whetham and Bradley J. Strawser. Boston: Brill Nijhoff, 169–195.

Frowe, Helen (2011). *The Ethics of War and Peace.* London: Routledge.

Gourley, Jim (2015). "The Military's Purpose Isn't to Break Things and Kill People, But It Should Be." *Foreign Policy* (24 September 2015). <http://foreignpolicy.com/2015/09/24/the-militarys-purpose-isnt-to-break-things-and-kill-people-but-it-should-be/>.

Hoffman, Bruce (2006). *Inside Terrorism.* Revised and expanded edition. New York: Columbia University Press.

Klay, Phil (2017). "What We're Fighting For." *New York Times* (10 February 2017).

Linn, Brian (2009). *The Echo of Battle: The Army's Way of War.* Cambridge, MA: Harvard University Press.

MacIntyre, Alasdair (2016). *Ethics in the Conflicts of Modernity: An Essay on Desire, Practical Reasoning, and Narrative.* New York: Cambridge University Press.

MacIntyre, Alasdair (2007). *After Virtue: A Study in Moral Theory.* 3rd ed. Notre Dame: University of Notre Dame Press.

Mattis, James (2008). "USJFCOM Commander's Guidance on Effects-Based Operations." *Joint Force Quarterly*, Vol. 51 (4th Quarter 2008), 105–108.

McMahan, Jeff (2005). "Just Cause for War." *Ethics and International Affairs*, Vol. 9, no. 3 (December 2005), 1–21.

McMaster, H.R. (2008). "On War: Lessons To Be Learned." *Survival*, Vol. 50, no. 1 (March 2008), 19–30.

Morris, Errol (2003). "The Fog of War: Eleven Lessons from the Life of Robert S. McNamara." Documentary. Sony Pictures Classics.

Oakeshott, Michael (1962). *Rationalism in Politics.* London: Methuen.

Orend, Brian (2013). *The Morality of War.* 2nd ed. Toronto: Broadview Press.

Orend, Brian (2001). "A Just War Critique of Realism and Pacifism." *Journal of Philosophical Research*, Vol. XXVI, 435–477.

Pickstock, Catherine (1998). *After Writing.* Malden, MA: Blackwell Publishers.

Reo, Nicholas James and Kyle Powys Whyte (2012). "Hunting and Morality as Elements of Traditional Ecological Knowledge." *Human Ecology*, Vol. 40, no. 1 (February 2012), 15–27.

Rodin, David (2004). "Terrorism without Intention." *Ethics*, 114 (July 2004), 752–771.

Ross, Janell (2015). "Mike Huckabee Says the Military's Job Is to 'Kill People and Break Things.' Well, Not Quite." *The Washington Post* (7 August 2015).

Schofield, John M. (1881). "Notes on 'The Legitimate in War.'" *Journal of the Military Service Institution*, Vol. 2, 1–10.

Schoonhoven, Richard (2010). "Invincible Ignorance, Moral Equality, and Professional Obligation." *Empowering Our Military Conscience: Transforming Just War Theory and Military Moral Education.* Ed. Roger Wertheimer. New York: Routledge, 107–129.

Shay, Jonathan (1994). *Achilles in Vietnam: Combat Trauma and the Undoing of Character.* New York: Scribner.

Tacitus, Publius Cornelius (c. 98 CE). *The Works of Tacitus: The Oxford Translation, Revised with Notes.* Vol. 2. London: Bell and Daldy (1872).

United Nations. "Declaration on Measures to Eliminate International Terrorism." Annex to UN General Assembly Resolution 49/60, "Measures to Eliminate International Terrorism." (9 December 1994). <https://www.un-.org/documents/ga/res/49/a49r060.htm>.

US Armed Forces. Joint Publication 3-0, *Operations* (Washington, DC: Joint Staff, September 2006); superseded in August 2011, then again in January 2017.

Van Buren, Peter (2011). *We Meant Well: How I Helped Lose the Battle for the Hearts and Minds of the Iraqi People.* New York: Metropolitan Books.

Vego, Milan (2009). "Systems versus Classical Approach to Warfare." *Joint Force Quarterly*, Vol. 52 (1st Quarter 2009), 40–48.

Walzer, Michael (2015). *Just and Unjust Wars: A Moral Argument with Historical Illustrations.* 5th ed. Philadelphia: Basic Books.

Weinstein, Adam (2017). "No, We Can't Kill Our Way To Victory Despite What 2 Misguided Lieutenant Colonels Might Think." *Task and Purpose* (8 December 2017). <https://taskandpurpose.com/no-cant-kill-way-victory-despite-2-misguided-lieutenant-colonels-might-think/>.

Wood, David (2016). *What Have We Done: The Moral Injury of Our Longest Wars.* New York: Little, Brown and Company, digital edition.

Notes

1 Capizzi (2015, 108–109).
2 Augustine was the first advocate for right intention; see *The City of God* (426 CE). Aquinas lists right intention as one of his three principles governing war (1485, II-II q. 40 a. 1 and q. 64 a. 3).

3 Daniel Bell marks the beginning of this dim view with Hugo Grotius (2009, 56–58).
4 For example, see McMahan (2005). For arguments against the dismissal of right intention, see Capizzi (2015, 71–126); Burkhardt (2017); and Bell (2009, 153–158).
5 For a brief summary of this trend, see Orend (2013, 18–24).
6 Coates (2016, 1–18).
7 Ibid., 12. Coates quotes Oakeshott (1962, 87, 84–85).
8 Coates' concern with the strictly rule-based approach in military ethics is a corroborating instance of Alasdair MacIntyre's concern with a modern moral framework that attempts an exhaustive "Grand Unified Theory" of morality; see MacIntyre (2016, 268).
9 Orend (2013, 21–24).
10 Recall David Wood's observation from Chapter 1: "Those we send to war are … given no opportunity or encouragement to think about or to discuss what makes some killings moral and others a sin or even illegal" (2016, ch. 11).
11 Orend (2013, 111); Bell (2009, 8).
12 Bell (2009, 73–88).
13 Coates (2016, 14).
14 In this regard, the modern rule-based approach to morality shares the deficiency many have leveled at the Catholic manualist tradition in its attempt to exhaustively codify morality. My thanks to Luis Pinto de Sa for this connection.
15 MacIntyre (2007, 30).
16 Ibid., 25.
17 There are some exceptions to this general criticism that I acknowledge in Chapter 4.
18 Coates (2016, 15).
19 Ibid.
20 Coates (2016, 293); Capizzi (2015, 7).
21 Tacitus (c. 98 CE, 372).
22 Capizzi (2015, 9).
23 Robert McNamara transferred his highly quantitative approach from the car industry to his new role as Secretary of Defense (serving 1961–1968). However, a few years into the Vietnam conflict, he privately expressed doubts to President Johnson about its suitability. It is an insider's critique that historians have revealed relatively recently, due in part to the recent declassification of material. See Burns and Novick (2017), episode 6; and Morris (2003).
24 Ross (2015).
25 For a sample of the debate, see Matt Cavanaugh, "The Military's Purpose is not to Kill People and Break Things," *War on the Rocks* (26 August 2015); Jim Gourley, "The Military's Purpose Isn't to Break Things and Kill People, But It Should Be," *Foreign Policy* (24 September 2015).
26 CNN Politics (10 September 2008).
27 Bolgiano and Taylor (2017). For one dissenting opinion, see Weinstein (2017).

28 Bolgiano and Taylor (2017).
29 The degree and extent of this obligation vary with one's position and duties. Soldiers in the heat of combat should not be focused on what peace terms the opposing political leaders might accommodate. They should, however, remain attentive to the possibility of their enemy counterparts surrendering. The degree of obligation increases for those soldiers involved not in the heat of combat, but in the cooler endeavors of determining strategic objectives, planning the campaigns to secure those objectives, and assessing the war's progress.
30 Capizzi (2015, 121).
31 I take these two subhuman categories, "base, as an animal or insect, or evil, as a monster or demon," from Brough (2007, 160).
32 Wood (2016, ch. 1).
33 This comparison to surgery comes from Orend (2013, 112), and Aquinas (1485, II-II q. 64 a. 3).
34 Schofield (1881; as cited by Linn 2009, 58).
35 Walzer (2015, 36).
36 Coplan (2011, 9).
37 Walzer (2015, 127).
38 I tackle the complexities of citizen-soldiers a bit further in Chapter 4, examining the military profession's customary deference to political leaders for judgments of *jus ad bellum*. I believe the deference is appropriate, just not absolute. I save the examination for that chapter because of the role deference can play in moral injury.
39 Brough (2007, 151).
40 Shay (1994, 103).
41 Ibid.
42 Walzer (2015, 138–143).
43 Holmes (1985, 368; as cited by Brough 2007, 157).
44 The pacifist response is to deny the latter – there can never be a duty to kill. While I part ways with the pacifist stance at a certain point, I share Brian Orend's concern that there can be an "embarrassing arrogance" in just war literature regarding pacifism (2001, 435–436). We all ought to have a commitment to nonviolent conflict resolution as a default. It is a *prima facie* commitment that even soldiers ought to maintain, understanding that their profession remains oriented on those circumstances that lie past the threshold of this commitment. Various situations require judging whether one is past that threshold or not. Counterinsurgencies, with no clear front lines, require this judgment of soldiers lower down the chain of command, despite it often being more difficult to make.
45 Brough (2007, 159).
46 Ibid., 160.
47 Ibid.
48 Ibid., 161.
49 Ibid. Another argument for a morally acceptable form of dehumanization is found in French and Jack (2015): they distinguish between animalistic dehumanization and mechanistic dehumanization, which correspond to Brough's subhumanization and nonhumanization, respectively.
50 Ibid.

51 Walzer suggests something similar about killing enemies when he states, "But the alienation [of the enemy] is temporary, the humanity imminent" (2015, 142).
52 Brough (2007, 163). The psychological research is that of Jonathan Shay and David Grossman, and moral injury is one of these repercussions.
53 Biggar (2013, 127).
54 French and Jack (2015, 180–181).
55 Shay's phrase from above.
56 Shay (1994, 103–120).
57 Ibid., 108–109.
58 Ibid.
59 Ibid., 29.
60 Ibid., 111, endnote 6. Shay cites Edith Hall's research in *Inventing the Barbarian* (New York: Oxford University Press, 1991).
61 Nor did it soften the victor's treatment of captured combatants and noncombatants. Both sides understood that if they fell in battle, they would be slaughtered, their towns plundered, and their families possessed as slaves. As awful as these actions might be, it did not stem from viewing the vanquished as subhuman. See Shay (1994, 103).
62 Shay (1994, 103, 111–120).
63 Ibid., 111.
64 Ibid., 112.
65 Ibid., 115.
66 Matthew 5:43–45; Luke 6:27–28, 35.
67 Augustine, Letter 138 (emphasis added).
68 Augustine, Letter 189.
69 Biggar (2013, 101).
70 Augustine, *Contra Faustum* XXII, 74.
71 I received another promising suggestion, though it requires more extensive study: the attitude toward prey within the hunting ethic of some indigenous American communities. In the practice of the Ojibwe, for example, a "hunter makes a speech of thankfulness to the animal/spirit world, showing appreciation in advance or after a harvest." Also: "Handling the deer carcass and disposing of unused portions should be done in a way that maintains dignity for the deer's spirit." See Reo and Whyte (2012, 15–27). While I hesitate to connect enemy soldiers with prey, the respectful attitude here seems in line with maintaining their humanity. Further research could confirm that the Ojibwe emphasize this attitude among their warriors doing battle with humans and not merely while hunting animals. My thanks to Monte Hoover for this reference.
    I would be remiss to not mention Shannon French's *The Code of the Warrior*, which summarizes the expectations for warriors across eight past and present cultures (see the second edition of 2017). Chapter 6, in fact, provides an account of some indigenous American communities, though not the Ojibwe above.
72 Klay (2017).
73 Ibid.
74 Ibid.
75 Aquinas (1485, II-II q. 64 a. 7).
76 Walzer (2015, 153).

77 Ibid. The moral relevance of this distinction is sometimes debated, but here I simply assume that it is relevant.
78 Walzer (2015, 155).
79 Ibid.
80 Ibid., 156.
81 Wood (2016, ch. 11).
82 Ibid., 132.
83 Dubik (2016, 18).
84 Ibid., 155.
85 Coates writes, "the problem is that the rule-based approach to the ethics of war is not just distinct from the traditional character-based approach. It is, typically, antagonistic towards it" (2016, 12). Coates later notes that "moral judgments [a reflective act] require the support of moral dispositions, feelings and inclinations [character traits]" (2016, 15).
86 It is important to emphasize that these are *default* stances – there are urgent war-waging decisions that require a honed instinct, just as there are war-fighting decisions that warrant careful reflection.
87 Dubik (2016, 141–143).
88 Ibid., 141–142.
89 Ibid., 142.
90 Shay (1994, 120).
91 US Armed Forces, Joint Publication 3-0, *Operations* (2006); superseded in 2011, then again in 2017. Neither of these subsequent editions include EBO.
92 Cheek (2002).
93 Pickstock (1998, xiii).
94 Vego (2009, 42).
95 McMaster (2008, 21).
96 Mattis (2008, 105–108).
97 Ibid., 106–107.
98 Ibid.
99 Van Buren (2011, 144).
100 James Willbanks (Burns and Novick 2017, episode 4).
101 Brough (2007, 151).

4 Empathy and Moral Injury

Given the nature of empathy as established in the second chapter, and the contributions empathy makes to the military profession as examined in the third chapter, it is now possible to address three lingering, interrelated issues: the general relation of empathy to moral injury, empathy's role in preventing moral injury, and empathy's role in recovering from moral injury.

In the first section below, I examine how the perception of others' humanity and their specific mental states puts empathy in the middle of the phenomenon of moral injury. This empathetic perception of others can set soldiers up for moral injury if they are not capable of assimilating it into their moral frameworks. In the second section, I argue that growing soldiers' moral understanding such that they can accomplish this assimilation is superior to the more common practice of merely telling them what, morally, they need to do and then expecting their obedience to shield them from moral burdens. Soldiers equipped with proper moral knowledge can integrate an empathetic understanding of others to maintain a right intention toward a just and lasting peace, thus preventing at least some occurrences of moral injury. Lastly, I spend the third section on how empathy can influence a soldier's struggle to overcome moral injury. On the one hand, a soldier may be hurt by the projective error that Dan Zahavi warns about with higher-level empathy (explained in the second chapter), especially given the isolation common to those morally injured. On the other hand, empathy free of this projective error proves vital for morally injured soldiers, since it can improve the soldier's self-knowledge, check tendencies toward self-condemnation, and enable processes of restoration and reconciliation. To explain these latter processes in relation to moral injury, I draw on Eleonore Stump's theory of atonement.

DOI: 10.4324/9781003248132-4

Empathy's Relation to Moral Injury

Recall the three routes to moral injury introduced in the first chapter: tragic betrayal, tragic right-doing, and tragic self-betrayal. In each of the cases illustrating these routes, the soldiers demonstrate appropriate moral emotions either before or after their respective military actions. Shay's Combat Infantry Badge recipient grieved the unwarranted deaths of the fishermen that he helped perpetrate. Romeo Dallaire recognized the humanity of the Rwandans and agonized over the loss of so many to genocide. Shay's seasoned soldier felt guilty because he grasped the Vietnamese infant's innocence that he breached in his protection of two comrades. Nik Rudolph struggled with killing a child soldier who might have been similarly blameless. John Lee acknowledged the basic humanity of the Nazi guards in his guilt and regret over summarily executing them. Undergirding all these moral emotions is an empathetic discernment of the humans involved. The emotions felt indicate the humanity perceived.

Empathy, therefore, contributes to moral injury in that it reveals the human status of others. It provides soldiers a greater moral awareness, and correspondingly, exposes them to grief that might otherwise not occur. However, to say that empathy contributes to moral injury is not to say that empathy is to *blame* for moral injury. Eyesight contributes to the sun's blinding glare and touch contributes to the burn from a hot stove, but these senses are not to blame for these harms. Nor is empathy to blame for the harm of moral injury. The blame is more appropriately placed on either the moral transgressions that prompt the moral emotions or the lack of moral understanding that hinders the soldiers from assimilating these emotions.

Furthermore, as I briefly suggested in the previous chapter, attempting to repress empathy can lead to moral injury. This risk is, metaphorically, the danger of holding one's breath too long, of interrupting the empathetic impulse and then stifling its return. The interruption may be appropriate and necessary in certain moments (the use of legitimate force, most prominently the killing act in combat; or the care of patients in an emergency room), but it can persist beyond its warrant. For soldiers, dehumanization or militarism may prolong the interruption; in coping with the regrettable duties of war, or preparing for them, they may dehumanize enemies and noncombatants or militaristically insist on the honor of soldiering to hide from the inherently tragic nature of any war. These efforts stave off their empathetic perception of others' humanity instead of addressing it. Yet avoiding the real import of one's actions eventually collapses to retrospective regret.[1] At this moment, even when soldiers' actions conform to moral principles, they may suffer moral injury because they recognize that their intentions did not. They recognize in themselves intentions that fall short of the moral obligation to intend a just and lasting peace. It is a form of tragic right-doing, in which they feel guilty despite no guilt-worthy actions.

Alternatively, attempting to repress empathy can spur moral injury because it leads to genuinely guilt-worthy actions (not merely immoral intentions). Moral and legal violations tend to accompany dehumanization and militarism, which all too easily take root in the absence of empathy. Instead of tragic right-doing, soldiers committing these guilt-worthy actions are exposed to the other forms of moral injury, tragic betrayal and tragic self-betrayal.

Empathy, then, is a conduit for the moral awareness that can prompt moral injury if soldiers are ill-equipped to handle it. A lack of empathy, however, invites a killing intention, dehumanization, and militarism, which not only spur moral injury among soldiers, but also war's atrocities. The best solution is to foster empathy to avoid the latter and better equip soldiers to process the moral awareness that empathy enhances.

Preventing Moral Injury

Dehumanizing others is sometimes justified as a way to prevent psychic pain, but it actually sets the conditions for such pain to occur retrospectively. This retrospective pain can lead to moral injury. Militarism is also sometimes defended as an attempt to protect soldiers from shame or guilt regarding their military duties, but this, too, lays the groundwork for moral injury. It makes soldiers susceptible to shock at the reality of their duties in contrast to the rousing, simplistic military recruitment messages and the "overwrought hero-worship of returning troops."[2] (This risk of moral injury is only one more reason to reject dehumanization and militarism; their instigation of wartime immorality is already widely recognized.) Soldiers must be prepared in some other way to deal with the moral and psychological vagaries of war.

Empathy helps since it counters dehumanizing and militaristic tendencies. As explained in the last chapter, empathy humanizes others in the midst of war's countervailing influences. Through lower-level empathy, a soldier perceives others as humans with various surface mental states and grasps some degree of what they are thinking or feeling. Through higher-level empathy, a soldier conceives of why they are thinking or feeling in these ways. Empathy thus keeps a soldier's moral awareness sharp, cognizant of fellow humans and their interior lives, instead of dulled by dehumanization or militarism.

However, empathetic perception can also contribute to moral injury if the soldier lacks the understanding necessary to accommodate it. This perception (somewhat like militarism above) can set the soldier up for shock at the reality of military duties – how incongruent they can be with her moral intuitions. It is this shock that motivates Wood's observation that I first shared in the introductory chapter:

> The US military has spent years and fortunes perfecting the most realistic and thorough combat training in the world. But in preparing young Americans for war, it has failed in one glaring aspect. Those we send to war are never trained to anticipate the moral quandaries of killing that they will face; they are given no opportunity or encouragement to think about or to discuss what makes some killings moral and others a sin or even illegal.[3]

Jonathan Shay echoes this sentiment:

> [Soldiers of all ranks] need training to perform effectively in the face of physical danger and to perform ethically in the face of moral danger. The relative proportions of physical and moral danger may tend to change according to rank, but in the interconnected modern world no enlisted man or woman [soldiers of lower rank] is too low to be released from moral strain or the need for moral understanding .... What service members need at every level is moral knowledge, as well as technical knowledge.[4]

Finally, Peter Kilner summarizes the problem thus: "there is a gap between what soldiers experience and what they are intellectually prepared to experience."[5] In interviews of over 350 soldiers and research spanning almost two decades, Kilner has found that few of them could answer two questions regarding the morality of war: How can war be morally justified? How can killing in war be morally justified?

Presumably, these questions are basic to a moral understanding of war. Yet, in all the training that soldiers complete, both in classroom settings and field exercises, the moral dimension of war is addressed too little. The training almost never includes discussions of these two questions. Moral expectations are communicated in military doctrinal manuals; written and verbal guidance from commanders in their orders, briefings, and regulations; predeployment briefings conducted by military lawyers regarding rules of engagement and other legal obligations; and sometimes in training scenarios and subsequent discussions, if the unit leaders address the topic. These moral expectations, however, are generally left as such, with no explanation of underlying principles for the soldiers to consider and incorporate into their moral comprehension of war. Soldiers are provided only a testimonial knowledge of what, morally, to do; not a deeper knowledge of why.[6] However, it is this deeper knowledge that soldiers need to assimilate their empathetic perceptions and corresponding moral awareness.

There are some minor exceptions to this general criticism: the US service academies (one source of its military officers) all mandate a core course in ethics, which includes several lessons devoted to the ethics of war. Other academy courses also address the moral evaluation of battlefield conduct. The Reserve Officer Training Corps (ROTC) program at college campuses, the source of most military officers, requires a few hours of instruction in military ethics that also move beyond the topic of rules to follow (barely).[7] The same is true of the third source of officers, Officer Candidate School (OCS). It is also important to recognize the education on ethics that occurs later in military careers at each service's professional development schools for commissioned and noncommissioned officers. These leaders are an authoritative group within the larger military population, so the investment in moral understanding is a meaningful one, but the investment is haphazard and insufficient. The point is even plainer with the enlisted majority of service members, who receive the least instruction in the moral dimension of war.[8]

Yet even in these possible exceptions, there remains the pedagogical risk of the instructors presenting the concepts as moral expectations and guidance, failing to develop the soldier's understanding of underlying principles. Choices affecting the class's style, curriculum, and accommodation of open-ended discussion can all steer the course toward rote training instead of education, toward moral testimony (communicating merely the instructor's own judgments and expecting students to master them) instead of moral understanding (fostering the soldier's ability to judge).[9]

As Kilner warns, "Moral injury occurs when soldiers are unable to reconcile their wartime experiences with their existing (i.e., peacetime) moral frameworks."[10] The above moral testimony can equip soldiers to take morally appropriate action in specific circumstances. It does not, however, aid the soldier in adapting to new circumstances, nor equip the soldier for the inevitable reflection after military action. It is in this reflection that a soldier experiences a "collision of the ethical beliefs they carried to war and the ugly realities of conflict" and is most susceptible to moral injury.[11] A soldier needs to be able to thoughtfully appraise her actions, not merely reiterate the guidance that led to them. The moral testimony that may have helped in the moment of decision proves no help in the process of reflection.

A well-developed moral understanding can alleviate a soldier's cognitive dissonance during reflection, particularly as prompted by empathy. Moral understanding aids the soldier in reconciling moral intuitions with war's demands instead of abandoning one or the other. Abandoning one's intuitions (including an intuitive regret for war) invites war crimes; abandoning war's demands invites the failure of achieving its legitimate ends. Developing a soldier's moral understanding refines both moral intuitions and her judgment on what the war effort actually requires.

Regardless of the results of her reflection, a soldier is better equipped to avoid moral injury with a refined moral understanding instead of mere testimony. If she assesses past actions as morally acceptable, she can grieve the necessity of the actions and yet grasp why they were necessary. Moral understanding equips her to justify actions, a practice inherent to being human (moral agents that we are).[12] It is a justification she needs to offer herself as much as to others. Even if a soldier's moral understanding results in assessing past actions as morally wrong, she is better equipped, conceptually, to cope with it. She can delineate more precisely how the action was wrong and who bears responsibility. She may feel guilt and sincerely be guilty of wrongdoing, but she is more capable of working through a process of acknowledgment, atonement, self-forgiveness, and related steps. She is not stuck concluding with some veterans that war simply insists that soldiers "push past immoral behavior" until "it becomes easier."[13]

Some Clarifications about Moral Testimony

At this point, I want to offer three clarifications regarding the need to foster moral understanding in soldiers instead of merely their obedience to moral testimony. The first clarification deals with moral advice. In the second clarification, I concede that there are moments of legitimate moral deference (deferring to the moral testimony of another). Lastly, I offer a larger concession to account for the customary deference in the military profession to political leaders regarding the overall justice of a war.

First, moral understanding can be spurred by moral advice; in this sense, moral judgments received from others are not problematic. It is only when those judgments are received uncritically (blindly, perhaps indifferently) that moral injury becomes a greater risk. Part of the concern above with current military training is that it does not include enough moral advice in training discussions, military schooling, or performance evaluations. Another problem is that in circumstances that warrant moral advice, the military leaders may, instead, communicate moral testimony as a decree. Military culture promotes strong personalities with a forceful demeanor, and these traits play an important role in proper military conduct. However, these traits can also undermine opportunities for fostering others' moral understanding. Military leaders should look for opportunities to provide subordinates advice instead of decrees. Of course, not every situation is amenable to this effort at growth through moral advice, but the opportunities are far more common than many hard-charging leaders recognize.

Unfortunately, moral advice will not always result in greater moral understanding, or there may be no time to grow it for some pressing decision. Therefore, the second clarification is that there are appropriate times for a soldier to defer to the moral testimony of another, accepting it as more authoritative than advice. In these moments, accepting the testimony is not blindly uncritical, but wise. Humans are subject to both epistemic and temperamental limitations, and the "responsible moral agent will want to do the right thing *more* than she will want to exhibit...moral understanding."[14] These limitations may vary with circumstances, an individual's abilities, an individual's dynamic mental and emotional states, and the availability of a trustworthy moral authority. It is to a soldier's moral credit if she recognizes her own inability to think quickly, her emotional turmoil of the moment (perhaps spurred by empathy), or her tendency toward recklessness and, consequently, attempts to overcome these shortcomings in particular situations through the moral testimony of another. In this way, "responsible moral deference is required of the virtuous person in some circumstances."[15] These moments of deference, however, should be minimized for at least two reasons. There is a greater risk of moral wrongdoing if the deferring moral agent habitually and robotically refrains from judgment. Also, the deferring moral agent is at greater risk of moral injury.

As a third clarification, I must address the distinct moral judgments of initiating war under the category of *jus ad bellum* and those judgments of conducting war falling under *jus in bello*. Specific *jus ad bellum* decisions are made by the most senior leaders in a nation-state's political system, and they are restricted to these individuals for morally respectable reasons. These judgments are one example of collective action that requires a qualification to the standard above of promoting moral understanding. As moral agents, soldiers require this understanding; yet as *limited* moral agents, they can responsibly defer to the judgment of political leaders regarding *jus ad bellum* considerations. This deference is not automatically morally permissible (even if, empirically, it is almost ubiquitous), especially for soldiers of a democracy who do not cease being citizens upon donning the uniform. They retain at least some version of the oversight responsibilities inherent to democratic practice.[16] The deference to senior leaders is provisional in nature, dependent upon their competence in making these *jus ad bellum* judgments, their trustworthiness in communicating these judgments, the plausibility of their judgments in specific circumstances, the urgency of those circumstances, and the access to relevant information.[17]

Moral deference is, therefore, unlike the epistemic deference that I grant to my car mechanic. Even if I come to suspect his testimony as unreliable, I will not educate myself on the proper operation and repair of my vehicle to form my own judgment, nor do I have an obligation to do so; I will seek the testimony of another mechanic. While I might similarly seek a second opinion regarding moral testimony on some matter, it is always with an eye toward the judgment falling back to me, because the actions corresponding to the judgment, or the relevant activities constitutive of collective action, falls to me. For moral deference to be appropriate, it must stem from an assessment of one's own limitations and the other's ability to render a proper moral judgment. We must approach moral deference from the starting point of our own judgment and action, shifting from this default only in light of relevant limitations. Moral deference is thus a "coping virtue," involving a concession to these limitations that are affecting one's own judgment.[18]

Epistemic deference, on the other hand, does not involve this same default that prioritizes my own judgment on the relevant matter in question.[19] The concession made in appealing to the epistemic expert's testimony is different than the concession made through the coping virtue of responsible moral deference. The epistemic concession carries no weight of unfulfilled personal responsibility, but the moral concession involves acknowledging some limitation that, if removed, would enable me to make the judgment that, ideally, I should. Even in moments of collective action, the agents of the action need to make a reasonable attempt at such judgment.

Thus, the division of moral labor that exists within the morality of war between *jus ad bellum* and *jus in bello* categories deserves a different term than "expert" for those who wield primary responsibility for making judgments within each category. Instead of moral experts who exercise similar authority as a car mechanic with a customer, we should recognize the unique deference involved with a term like moral "trustees." These trustees form moral judgments as part of collective action on matters that still fall under legitimate, even obligatory, scrutiny of other community members. A car mechanic's judgment is properly scrutinized by other car mechanics; a moral trustee's judgment should be scrutinized by a broader audience. The trustees' judgments are not testimony to be received uncritically. It is immoral to grant these trustees too much authority and a correspondingly irresponsible level of moral deference.[20] In other words, the obedience expected of soldiers appropriately involves "critical intention, deliberation, and decision," not unreflective acceptance.[21]

If political leaders are the trustees of *jus ad bellum*, then military personnel are the trustees of *jus in bello*. There is a reciprocal moral deference due to reciprocal limitations. The soldiers generally have greater epistemic access than the political leaders regarding the facts informing *jus in bello* judgments, as well as an urgency for decisions in those judgments. In addition, the soldiers have honed their epistemic abilities and temperament through military training and experience, which equips them to better fulfill *jus in bello* principles. These factors justify the provisional delegation of *jus in bello* judgments to the military. All the while, trustees of each moral category remain subject to the scrutiny of their fellow trustees and community members at large.

This discussion of epistemic vs. moral deference is meant to sketch the contours of war as a collective action. I suggest the notion of moral trusteeship to allow for the coexistence of moral understanding and moral deference in soldiers as responsible moral agents. The persistent difficulty is determining what specific circumstances call for in terms of a soldier exercising her own judgment or deferring to her superiors. In practice, soldiers are consistently absolved of responsibility in violations of the *jus ad bellum* category. The deference of soldiers to the moral judgments of political leaders that initiated wrongful wars is widely respected.[22] Given the nature of collective action, such deference seems unavoidable. If, however, we accept moral deference as a concession, it may be that soldiers enjoy too much leeway, especially those who are senior in rank and influence. The Nazi general Erwin Rommel, for example, is simultaneously praised for his enforcement of *jus in bello* principles in the European theater of World War II and decried for contributing so significantly to Hitler's violation of *jus ad bellum* principles that rule out such a war of aggression.[23] Rommel's position is where responsible moral deference is the most suspect because the division of moral labor is the least defensible. The cases get easier the more one travels down the military chain of command to personnel without the requisite combination of epistemic ability, temperament, experience, and information, or in the opposite direction to unambiguous members of political leadership plainly responsible for *jus ad bellum* judgments with no one to properly defer to.

These concessions to moments of legitimate moral deference do not remove the enduring need to foster a thorough moral understanding among soldiers. Soldiers need a grasp of *jus ad bellum* principles to fulfill their fundamental duties as a citizen, to fulfill their military duties in conducting the war's operations, and to provide themselves and others a moral justification for their actions, which helps to minimize moral injury. Lacking such understanding, soldiers will struggle to "contextualize or justify personal actions or the actions of others" and accommodate "these potentially morally challenging experiences into pre-existing moral schemas...."[24] These inadequate moral schemas contribute to two specific judgments that underly moral injury: the soldier's opinion regarding the moral status of his act, and his opinion regarding his responsibility for the act. Getting either judgment wrong can prompt moral injury; moral understanding that improves those judgments helps to prevent it.

Admittedly, greater moral understanding can make a soldier more susceptible to moral injury in at least one way. The soldier may evaluate the moral aspects of an international issue more accurately than the senior political leaders, to the point that the leaders' decision for war becomes an instance of tragic betrayal. One possible example, depending on the moral status of the 2003 invasion of Iraq, is the struggle of Navy officer Steven Dundas, who deployed to Iraq with full confidence in the justice and humanitarianism of the mission but "returned home broken." He explains,

> Seeing the devastation of Iraqi cities and towns, some of it caused by us, some by the insurgents and the civil war that we brought about, hit me to the core. I felt lied to by our senior leadership. And I felt those lies cost too many thousands of American lives and far too much destruction.[25]

This route to moral injury is a risk inherent to war (and to collective action, in general). This risk can be mitigated by the political leaders exercising the same level of moral understanding that I am recommending for soldiers. Even with the presence of this risk (mitigated or not), improving soldiers' moral understanding remains vital for the reasons above.

Some may think that moral understanding among soldiers is increasingly irrelevant due to expanding technological capabilities and the corresponding physical distance between soldier and target. Similarly, technology often mediates the identification and perception of enemy combatants through video feeds, thermal or infrared detection, or other sanitized portrayals. Such developments would seem to circumvent the empathetic perceptions that ground my argument for inculcating moral understanding in soldiers. However, such distance or mediation does not necessarily reduce enemies to objects (which is a problematic notion, anyway, as discussed in the prior chapter). William MacKenzie observes that drone pilots often experience a "remote intimacy" with targeted individuals such that there is an "empathic proximity where physical proximity is missing."[26] The pilots demonstrate our innate human tendency to "narrativize" actions to make sense of them. Despite physical distance or technological separation, empathetic perceptions will continue to occur, and therefore necessitate moral understanding for the health of military personnel and for the trustworthiness of their decisions.[27]

Overcoming Moral Injury

While occurrences of moral injury among soldiers would decrease if they possessed an improved understanding of war's moral dimension, it would be naïve to suggest that moral injury would disappear. War's tragic nature ensures that even in the most clearly justified wars, soldiers will struggle with the moral loss involved, and some will falter in that struggle. Soldiers caught up in wars with a murky justification will be even more vulnerable. Therefore, a consideration of the relationship between empathy and moral injury would not be complete without addressing empathy's impact on healing this "pervasive sense of taint."[28]

Scholars and health practitioners have increasingly advocated for a stronger distinction between post-traumatic stress disorder (PTSD) and moral injury.[29] One reason is the different therapies required due to their different causes. Theories of PTSD describe the struggle "of individuals *harmed by* others (and other unpredictable, uncontrollable, and threatening circumstances)," while moral injury refers to the struggle entailed by *harming* others.[30] PTSD is rooted in fear and subconscious survival mechanisms. Moral injury is rooted in grief, guilt, shame, and betrayal. It is "a species of emotional and psychological pain that takes one's agency as its object...."[31] Pain stemming from one's agency, however, can be a unique challenge to modern psychologists and counselors. As Bernard Verkamp highlights, there is an inappropriate fit between soldiers' grief and guilt and most modern medical therapies.[32] These therapies often attempt to deny or dismiss the grief and guilt, treating them only as maladaptive neuroses. "Psychotherapists are often too eager to relieve guilt, and, thereby, undermine the patient's need to feel remorseful."[33]

In contrast, Verkamp notes premodern practices of penance for soldiers, even for those who fought on the side considered just.[34] Such practices demonstrate a recognition of the tragedy and moral loss of war, regardless of its justification. Verkamp argues that such practices also illustrate how guilt can be a guide and grief can be a virtue, contrary to modern trends. In line with Verkamp, as well as other recent scholarship on moral injury, I want to suggest that all soldiers, especially those morally injured, should be encouraged and equipped to lament the tragedy of their warring actions through something like atonement.[35] Whether involved in an immoral action or not, some kind of moral restoration is necessary.

The Need for Atonement

It is regrettable that war must be chosen at all. Morally injured soldiers wrestle with this truth, which makes the occurrence of moral injury somewhat commendable. It reflects a functioning conscience. Even when morally justified, war is a concession to nonideal conditions, a necessary compromise, and a tragedy. In the words of Tobias Winright and Ann Jeschke, "Even when war might be morally justified and fought justly, we think there is need of restoration and reconciliation for returning warriors."[36] Specifically, soldiers need the sense of their own goodness restored and their affiliation with that goodness reconciled. Soldiers suffering from moral injury are caught in the grip of this need. As Eleonore Stump points out, the term "atonement" originally referred to this restoration and reconciliation, a "setting at one...after discord or strife."[37] While the term has acquired an unfortunate connotation of punishment and sacrifice to "[placate] an offended God,"[38] its meaning of setting at one, or restoring unity, is key to overcoming moral injury.

Right away, I want to address a potential confusion. Atonement refers to setting at one after "discord or strife," which normally means that a wrong has been done. However, moral injury is not a simple wrong done, at least in two of the three types that I have defined. In

tragic betrayal, there is a moral wrong, but it is instigated by someone else and the soldier is unwittingly involved. She is materially, but
not morally, responsible, as illustrated in my first chapter with Shay's
CIB recipient and the case of Romeo Dallaire. In the type of moral
injury that I call tragic right-doing, the soldier has not committed a
wrong (recall Shay's seasoned soldier and Nik Rudolph). There has
been harm but no injustice, and therefore, the action has effects wor-
thy of grief but not of guilt. Instead of a "setting at one after a wrong
done," soldiers of these two categories need a "setting at one after another's injustice, or a justified harm, has been done." In either case,
"discord" remains a suitable term for that which necessitates restoration. In tragic betrayal, the material responsibility for the wrong generates discord between a soldier's presumption of her own goodness
and the badness of the action she carried out. In tragic right-doing,
the harm caused by her justified action generates discord between her
knowledge that she did no wrong and the grief she feels over the effects
of her action.[39] Therefore, I stick with "atonement" as defined above
to refer to the moral restoration required in cases of tragic betrayal
and tragic right-doing.

In the third category of moral injury, tragic self-betrayal, a soldier
betrays his own moral convictions such that he is morally and materially responsible for a wrong done (recall the example of John Lee).
This dissonance between moral conviction and immoral action con-
forms with the more customary sense of "discord" as moral wrongdoing. Thus, atonement straightforwardly applies.

The crucial question across all three categories of moral injury is
identifying what needs to be set at one. What is the unity that has
been broken? It involves the soldier's intellect and will and the soldier's
assessment of his action and its effects. The tragedy inherent to war
can prompt soldiers to doubt both their ability to identify the good
and doubt their inclination toward goodness. It is easy for a soldier
to doubt his intellect, since it is often difficult to identify the good secured through the harm he caused. Or, the good secured may seem remote or small compared to the immediacy or scale of the harm. Or, the
supposed good evaporates in the discovery of betrayal. In these ways,
the soldier may become convinced that he is defective in his judgments
about the good. Similarly, it is easy for a soldier to doubt his own will,
since he *did* intend the harm that he caused, at the very least in con-
ceding to his own participation in war. In the heat of battle, especially,
he may have celebrated some harm he inflicted because, let's sup-
pose, it was a victorious moment in which he successfully protected

his comrades. Reflecting on the harm and the feelings surrounding it, however, may cause him to question his own devotion to the good.

These doubts of both intellect and will introduce an internal, psychic fragmentation for the soldier. This fragmented sense of self marks one half of the moral injury that must be remedied. One can readily see this fragmented sense of self in each of the cases described in the first chapter. The soldiers harbor concerns about their discernment of the good and their commitment to the good. However, because we are considering a morally respectable soldier – at least, one whose conscience is not silent – then his intellect and will are, in one sense, not the primary issue. The soldier's grief and guilt are a vindication that his intellect and will *are* oriented on the good. As one study states:

> inherent [to] moral injury is the supposition that anguish, guilt, and shame are signs of an intact conscience and self- and other-expectations about goodness, humanity, and justice. In other words, [moral] injury is only possible if acts of transgression produce dissonance (conflict), and dissonance is only possible if the service member has an intact moral belief system.[40]

The harm that a soldier causes, however, can act on his properly oriented intellect and will to generate a lingering uneasiness, a vague dirtiness, that also contributes to the soldier's feelings of grief and guilt. As introduced in the first chapter, even if the soldier believes his actions were justified, he still may strain to reconcile them with their harmful effects. The memory of the harm can haunt him and come to resemble what Aquinas called a "stain on the soul...a certain privation of the soul's brightness."[41] As Stump elaborates, this stain is a residue of past wrongdoing that remains with the person in the present, beyond any defects in the intellect or will.[42]

This moral residue is the other half of moral injury. However, this claim requires clarification because grounding moral injury in a stain on the soul indicates the soldier has committed some wrongdoing. Cases of tragic self-betrayal meet this condition; the soldier struggled with a complex moral decision and chose wrongly. In cases of tragic betrayal, wrongdoing remains present, but the moral culpability lies with the soldier's superiors. His participation alone, though, is enough to generate a different version of this moral residue. We can call this version a stain on the soldier's life instead of his soul, which helps to indicate the external source of wrongdoing; it did not stem from the soldier's own will.[43]

In tragic right-doing, no wrongdoing is actually present. To help identify the moral residue pertinent to this type, I want to draw upon Philip Hallie's perspective of his participation in World War II.[44] As he researched accounts of resistance to the Holocaust several years after the war, Hallie discovered the activity of Le Chambon, a southern French village that protected thousands of Jewish individuals. Led by their Protestant pastor, the villagers took Jewish adults and children into their homes and hid them under the guise of a longstanding international school. The escapees took on the role of teacher or student. For Hallie, the most interesting aspect was that the villagers maintained a strict pacifist policy. They refused to forcefully resist the French Vichy government. While the pastor and other village leaders were imprisoned on occasion for violating Vichy's policies, they were (inexplicably) released. Hallie and the villagers he interviewed point out that forceful resistance would have triggered a prompt and crushing response, as had occurred in other parts of France. Hallie wrestled with the village's pacifist strategies that contrasted with the violence of his own military service:

> I had been a combat artilleryman in the European theater and I knew that decent killers like me had done more to prevent the mass murders from continuing than this pacifist mountain village had done. And so I found myself wavering between praising military valor above all and praising moral valor above all...
>
> I realized that for me too the little story of Le Chambon is grander and more beautiful than the bloody war that stopped Hitler. I do not regret fighting in that war – Hitler had to be stopped, and he had to be stopped by killing many people. The war was necessary. But my memories of it give me only a sullied joy because in the course of the three major battles I participated in, I saw the detached arms and legs and heads of young men lying in blood-stained snow. The story of Le Chambon gives me unsullied joy. Why?[45]

Hallie's answer to this question employs the biblical story of the flood and subsequent rainbow. The ancient flood had wiped out mankind, which had become extremely corrupt and violent. Afterward, the rainbow became a symbol of God's restraint, which Hallie applies to the village:

> And the reason the rainbow is closer to my heart than the Flood that was World War II is that the people of Le Chambon helped

without harming, saved lives without torturing and destroying other lives. This is why the rainbow gives me unsullied joy and necessary and useful killing does not.[46]

Hallie is confident in the rightness of his military service, even though he is also grieved by it. He settles on "sullied joy" to accommodate this tension between the rightness of his action and the harm of its effects. This tension can prove difficult to reconcile for many soldiers and spurs cases of moral injury. For Shay's seasoned soldier and Nik Rudolph, the sullied nature of their actions overshadows any joy, which I take to mean the knowledge and gratification of the rightness of their actions. They grieve the harm they caused to the point of doubting the rightness of their conduct. Alternatively, a soldier may suppress his emotional capacity for grief to cling to the rightness of his act. Resolving the tension in this direction invites one's confidence to reify into obstinance, thoughtlessness, or callousness. Hallie's "sullied joy" is the appropriate resolution. It requires the moral understanding of war explored earlier, particularly the recognition of tragedy in one's forceful actions. It is this sulliedness, or tarnish, of some right actions that describes the moral residue of tragic right-doing.

In summary, the unity that has been broken in a morally injured soldier consists of two aspects: first, a fragmented sense of self such that the soldier doubts the orientation of his intellect and will toward the good, which is prompted by grief and the felt guilt of moral injury (whether genuinely guilty or not); and second, a moral residue generated by committing a significant harm (whether also an injustice or not), or participating in such harm, or even merely witnessing such harm. The moral residue changes with the type of moral injury at hand: tragic self-betrayal produces a stain on the soul of a soldier, in line with Aquinas' analysis of culpably committing a moral wrong; tragic betrayal produces a stain on the life of a soldier, stemming from innocently participating in a moral wrong; and tragic right-doing produces a tarnish that results from the tragedy inherent to some right actions. (There is also moral right-doing that is not tragic, producing Hallie's unsullied joy; too many soldiers see war in this light.)

Atonement, particularly Stump's conception of it, can provide the moral restoration required to overcome these two aspects of moral injury. Stump identifies repentance as the part of atonement that remedies the first aspect, the "defective states of the wrongdoer's intellect and will."[47] Stump notes that a repentant person will want to "help remedy the damage she did in the world."[48] A morally injured soldier is not necessarily a wrongdoer, given cases of tragic right-doing and tragic betrayal, but in these cases, repentance remains relevant because the soldier has done something involving moral loss, something nonideal even if permissible, and he needs to recognize this feature of his action. As I argued in the previous chapter, war is commonly and naïvely viewed as an unqualified good by American military culture and the communities to which American soldiers return. In actuality, war in even its most justified form is tragic; it "is the realm of the paradoxical: the morally repugnant is the morally permissible, and even the morally necessary."[49] A morally injured soldier experiences this truth. He can relieve his fragmented sense of self through an effort at repenting, or making amends, for the harm done, even if no injustice is involved. Making amends is difficult for soldiers given that their harms are often impossible to directly rectify or repair (even more so if their war was in a distant land). Where direct reparation is impossible, a person can still "contribute to good wherever she can" to demonstrate to others and herself (perhaps most important for the morally injured) that she is truly committed to the good.[50]

Stump's point is reinforced by psychologists who have worked extensively with morally injured soldiers. As part of therapy, Bret Litz and his co-authors recommend "exposure to corrective life experience." They explain that this experience...

> entails increasing the accessibility of positive judgments about the self by doing good deeds and positive judgments about the world by seeing others do good deeds .... This counters self-expectations of moral inadequacy and the experience of being tainted by various acts.[51]

Along these same lines, nonprofit organizations like Team Rubicon and The Mission Continues seek to assist veterans by engaging them in philanthropic activities, helping them to "find purpose through community impact."[52] These "corrective life experiences" are conceptually analogous to repentance or making amends.

Even if a morally injured soldier gains greater confidence in his orientation toward the good (in both intellect and will), he may yet remain haunted by the memory of his troubling war actions. This moral residue is the second aspect of moral injury. In order to deal with this residue, Stump distinguishes between different notions of remembering. She states, "A person may remember *that* he was born in Chicago, but his doing so is different from his remembering *being* born in Chicago..."[53] The first kind of remembering is of a propositional nature, while the second kind retains an "in the present" reliving of the memory. Stump explains that a wrongdoer can overcome the stain on the soul by shifting the memory of harm done from the emotionally charged kind to the propositional kind. Stump calls this shift a type of forgetting, in that the past action remains a cognition, but it loses its "emotional coloring."[54] (Stump argues that only this nuanced forgetting makes sense regarding past wrongs; literally losing all memory of them is an act of self-deception and a further injury to the victim.[55])

This shift in memory is also an important moment for the morally injured soldier dealing with a stain on her soul, a stain on her life, or the tarnish of tragic right action. While her past actions are not necessarily wrong (depending on the type of moral injury), they are still painful due to the harm that she caused, participated in, or witnessed. She needs to be able to forget her past actions not through losing all knowledge of them, but in Stump's sense of losing their felt characteristic. In this manner, the past actions remain with the soldier as propositional knowledge, but they lose their morally injurious grip.

Triggering this shift to "propositional memory" is a key topic of research among those working with morally injured soldiers. Many suggest these soldiers make the shift through recrafting their own narratives in a way that accommodates the harms they caused.[56] Stump makes a similar point when discussing wrongdoing: this shift to propositional memory can occur when the wrongdoer repents, the victim forgives, and the wrong becomes "part of their ongoing joint story of mutual love and care."[57] Moral injury among soldiers is more difficult because the victims cannot usually participate in such a reconciliation. This absence is another reason soldiers may find moral injury so intractable, and it underscores the need for their communities' involvement, which may serve as a partial and limited surrogate for those they harmed, at least in terms of providing them an audience for atoning efforts. Moral injury cannot be healed alone.[58]

Empathy's Impact on Atonement

Stump's notion of atonement, composed of repentance and a shift to propositional memory, provides a therapeutic framework for soldiers overcoming moral injury. This framework is reinforced by recent scholarship among psychologists, counselors, and philosophers. With this conception of atonement in place, I can now address empathy's impact on it, and therefore, empathy's role in overcoming moral injury. Empathy's impact is due largely to its influence on a person's self-knowledge. Edith Stein notes that empathetically grasping another's experience can include the other's experience of oneself:

"through my experience of others I can precisely come to attain a new experience of myself .... I can come to adopt an alienating attitude towards myself and thereby come to see myself as others see me."[59] This empathetic self-knowledge is a central reason soldiers require a supportive, caring community to overcome moral injury. They need this "alienation" from themselves to interrupt their self-condemning attitudes and introduce the possibility of a new, healthier self-perspective.

In repenting, it is through empathy's feedback that a soldier can come to see himself in a better light and repair his fragmented sense of self. For example, Litz and his colleagues note that the "perception of forgiveness from others [positively] affected self-forgiveness over time."[60] If a soldier is isolated from others, however, the projective error of higher-level empathy can exacerbate self-doubt and self-condemnation. I introduced this error in the second chapter to highlight the risk of projecting one's own views onto others. Moral injury illustrates the damage done when those projected views are self-condemning, remain uncorrected, and take on the weight and credibility of others' judgments (even if imagined and unsubstantiated). Isolated, the soldier presumes others feel about him and his past actions the way that he himself does.

In the actual presence of supportive others, the soldier's lower-level empathetic input can counter the higher-level projective error.[61] In providing this support, it is important to note that others should not deny, trivialize, or rationalize the harm or injustice done by the soldier. The soldier needs to empathize with others who simultaneously acknowledge the moral loss and the soldier's goodness, since this integrated view of himself is what the soldier must achieve. As Litz et al. state:

> [Soldiers need to] process the event in a way so that accommodation, but not *over-accommodation*, can occur. Rather than coping with a morally injurious event by denying it or excessively accommodating it, what is needed is a new synthesis – a new way to view the world and the self in it that takes into account the reality of the event and its significance without giving up too much of what was known to be good and just about the world and the self prior to the event (and what can be revealed in the future) .... One does not need to accept the act to accept the imperfect self that committed the act.[62]

Another component of avoiding this projective error of higher-level empathy is humility. Humility underscores the limits of the soldier's control in the morally troubling situation, which helps to reduce the perceived incompatibility between his troubling action and the orientation of his intellect and will toward the good. Humility also improves self-knowledge, in that it helps a soldier be more open to the empathetic feedback drawn from supportive others. Mark Wilson articulates the point well:

> There are no perfect sightlines for a vision of the self. Humility calls for both a rigorous honesty in the interpretation of memory, and a realism with regard to the limits of self-awareness and the traps of self-deception. It also, not incidentally, opens us outward to others in the realization that as social beings we know ourselves in relation, and thus the search for self-knowledge is a communal activity, necessitating the participation of friends, spouses, fellow veterans, counselors, and the civic body at large.[63]

Overcoming the moral residue of war's forceful actions is different than the fragmented sense of self. While both require a supportive community, the latter calls for repentance with its focus on doing good (and seeing others do good). The former calls for a shift in the soldier's memory that frees him from the past such that he can regain hope in being good. Empathy can contribute to this shift to propositional memory of the morally injurious event, if the soldier can empathize with a trusted and supportive community that listens well. The work on this half of moral injury is composed of discussion more than action, and this imperative to listen to soldiers resonates across the moral injury literature. "So before analyzing, before classifying, before thinking, before trying to *do* anything – we should *listen*."[64]

It is also important to note that empathy can interfere with this shift to propositional memory. Empathy is, by definition, grasping the felt characteristic of an experience. If it makes sense that one can empathize with one's past self – accessing what those past circumstances felt like – then empathy can get in the way of remembering those circumstances in a propositional manner without its original "emotional coloring." Therefore, soldiers who are naturally more empathetic are more susceptible to the moral residue that can trigger moral injury. The answer to this concern also lies in community. With the help of others, the soldier can "draw a firm line around the past and its related associations, so that the mistakes of the past do not define the present and the future ...."[65] Coupled with genuine and repeated acts of repentance and benevolence, the soldier can cultivate a sense of his present self that is increasingly different than his past convictions. Such work requires time and persistence; as Jonathan Shay observes from his work, "Recovery is much more like training for a marathon than a miracle faith healing."[66]

Empathy, then, contributes to a morally injured soldier's improvement by enabling the process of atonement and the moral restoration it entails. Only with empathetic self-knowledge can a soldier escape the self-condemning attitudes stemming from his fragmented sense of self and the moral residue of past actions; further, this empathy can only occur in the presence of others who actively and effectively support him.

Conclusion

I began this argument for empathy's relevance to the military profession by identifying two sources of confusion: one regarding the nature of empathy and another regarding the nature of soldiering. I spent the second chapter on empathy, summarizing four conceptions of it and then offering a provisional definition that ruled out one conception (theory-theory) and integrated aspects of the remaining three (simulation theory, direct perception theory, and narrative theory). I then shifted to soldiering, arguing that the heart of the practice is contributing to a just and lasting peace. The necessity for a right intention among soldiers toward this peace is a deficiency in contemporary accounts of *jus in bello*; empathy helps soldiers to sustain this intention.

Even if empathy helps in this manner, I have considered in this chapter whether empathy makes soldiers more vulnerable to moral injury. Empathy does contribute to moral injury in that it underscores the moral loss involved in even the justified actions of war. However, empathy is not therefore to blame as the cause of moral injury; empathy's role resembles that of our physical senses in physical injury. Just as hearing is not to blame for loud noises resulting in deafness, so empathy is not to blame for debilitating grief or guilt. Dehumanization, militarism, and a killing intention are the real culprits. Because empathy promotes a genuinely moral intention of peacemaking instead of warmongering, it can help to prevent at least several moments of moral injury. Some morally injured soldiers suffer from a recognition of their own intentions that fall short of establishing a just peace. Other morally injured soldiers suffer from the betrayal of superiors who harbor similarly poor intentions.

Instead of suppressing the empathetic impulse to the point of deadening one's moral sense, only to be haunted by it later, empathy and the awareness it provides needs to be better accommodated in military education and training. Soldiers need to understand why their actions are morally permissible (or not), instead of merely what actions are morally permissible. Such understanding would enable soldiers to assimilate empathetic input instead of being anguished by it. In sum, I have argued for both a certain disposition in soldiers (enabled by empathy) and the moral understanding of war to complement it. The two reinforce each other: right intent spurs reflective thought, which improves the soldier's discernment of that which fulfills right intent.

The empathetic soldier is at once more competent, more vulnerable, and unavoidable in important ways. She is more competent due to her superior understanding of humans and the basic respect entailed by empathy. She is more vulnerable in that she is more aware of the tragedy and grief inherent to war, no matter its justice. Third, she is unavoidable in two senses: in a practical sense due to involuntary lower-level empathy and habitual higher-level empathy; and in an aspirational sense, given the humanizing influence of empathy and the intention toward a just and lasting peace that it promotes. The empathetic soldier is, therefore, both an ideal and an obligation.

Works Cited

Aquinas, Thomas (1485). *Summa theologiae.* Trans. Fathers of the English Dominican Province. Second and Revised Edition, 1920. Online Edition Copyright © 2008 by Kevin Knight. <http://www.newadvent.org/summa/>.

Burkhardt, Todd (2017). *Just War and Human Rights: Fighting with Right Intention.* Albany, NY: SUNY Press.

Driver, Julia (2015). "Virtue and Moral Deference." *Ethics and Politics*, Vol. 17, no. 2, 27–40.

Driver, Julia (2013). "Moral Expertise: Judgment, Practice, and Analysis." *Social Philosophy and Policy*, Vol. 30, no. 1–2, 280–296.

Gusterson, Hugh (2016). *Drone: Remote Control Warfare.* Cambridge, MA: MIT Press.

Hallie, Philip (1979). *Lest Innocent Blood Be Shed.* New York: HarperCollins (1994).

Hills, Alison (2012). *The Beloved Self: Morality and the Challenge from Egoism.* New York: Oxford University Press.

Howsepian, Avak Albert (2016). "Helping PTSD Sufferers." CareLeader.org. <https://www.careleader.org/helping-ptsd-victims/>.

Kilner, Peter (2016). "Military Leaders' Role in Mitigating Moral Injury," blog article (11 November 2016). <http://soldier-ethicist.blogspot.com/2016/11/the-military-leaders-role-in-mitigating.html>.

Litz, Brett T., Nathan Stein, Eileen Delaney, Leslie Lebowitz, William P. Nash, Caroline Silva, and Shira Maguen (2009). "Moral Injury and Moral Repair in War Veterans: A Preliminary Model and Intervention Strategy." *Clinical Psychology Review*, Vol. 29, 695–706.

MacKenzie, William A. IV (2017). "A 'Human Endeavor:' Killing in Contemporary US Combat Narratives." Master's thesis, Department of English, University of Mississippi.

Meagher, Robert Emmet and Douglas A. Pryer, eds. (2018). *War and Moral Injury: A Reader*. Eugene, OR: Cascade Books.

Orend, Brian (2013). *The Morality of War*. 2nd ed. Toronto: Broadview Press.

Osiel, Mark (1998). "Obeying Orders: Atrocity, Military Discipline, and the Law of War." *California Law Review*, Vol. 86, no. 5, 939–1128.

Ryle, Gilbert (1957). "On Forgetting the Difference between Right and Wrong." *Essays in Moral Philosophy*. Ed. AI Melden. Seattle: University of Washington Press, 154–167.

Schoonhoven, Richard (2010). "Invincible Ignorance, Moral Equality, and Professional Obligation." *Empowering Our Military Conscience: Transforming Just War Theory and Military Moral Education*. Ed. Roger Wertheimer. New York: Routledge, 107–129.

Shanks Kaurin, Pauline (2020). *On Obedience: Contrasting Philosophies for the Military, Citizenry, and Community*. Annapolis, MD: Naval Institute Press.

Shay, Jonathan (2014). "Moral Injury." *Psychoanalytic Psychology*, Vol. 31, no. 2, 182–191.

Shay, Jonathan (2002). *Odysseus in America: Combat Trauma and the Trials of Homecoming*. New York: Scribner.

Shay, Jonathan (1994). *Achilles in Vietnam: Combat Trauma and the Undoing of Character*. New York: Scribner.

Sherman, Nancy (2015). *Afterwar: Healing the Moral Wounds of our Soldiers*. New York: Oxford University Press.

Singer, Peter (1972). "Moral Experts." *Analysis*, Vol. 32, no. 4, 115–117.

Stump, Eleonore (2018). *Atonement*. New York: Oxford University Press.

Verkamp, Bernard (1993). *The Moral Treatment of Returning Warriors in Early Medieval and Modern Times*. Scranton: University of Scranton Press.

Walzer, Michael (2015). *Just and Unjust Wars: A Moral Argument with Historical Illustrations*. 5th ed. New York: Basic Books.

Wiinikka-Lydon, Joseph (2018). "Dirty Hands and Moral Injury." *Philosophy*, Vol. 93, no. 3, 355–374.

Wilson, Mark (2014). "Moral Grief and Reflective Virtue." *Virtue and the Moral Life: Theological and Philosophical Perspectives*. Eds. William Werpehowski and Kathryn Getek Soltis. Lanham, MD: Lexington Books, 57–73.

Winright, Tobias and E. Ann Jeschke (2015). "Combat and Confession: Just War and Moral Injury." *Can War Be Just in the 21st Century? Ethicists Engage the Tradition*. Eds. Tobias Winright and Laurie Johnston. Maryknoll, NY: Orbis Books, 169–187.

Wood, David (2016). *What Have We Done: The Moral Injury of Our Longest Wars*. New York: Little, Brown and Company, digital edition.

Wood, David (2014). "Moral Injury: The Grunts." *Huffington Post* (18 March 2014). <http://projects.huffingtonpost.com/projects/moral-injury/the-grunts>.

Notes

1 Joseph Wiinikka-Lydon observes, "There is a shock, even a break, to moral injury where the way one had understood the moral ecology of the world prior to their injurious experience is found retrospectively to be incorrect" (2018, 360). Similarly, Mark Wilson notes the "reflective suffering" of soldiers as they process troubling situations (2014, 61).

2 Wood (2016, ch. 1).

3 Ibid., ch. 11.

4 Shay (2002, 223, 224).

5 Kilner (2016).

6 I am indebted to Alison Hills (2012) and Julia Driver (2015) for their work on moral testimony.

7 To its credit, the ROTC program at Texas A&M University mandates a semester-long ethics course. My thanks to Jon Thompson for pointing out this exception.

8 I draw these facts from my own experience; they are also corroborated by Burkhardt (2017, 37–38).

9 I would be remiss if I did not recognize the efforts of the US Army's Center for the Army Profession and Ethic, which led a campaign for greater clarity and attention on the professional ethic that ought to ground military service and the development of soldiers' moral understanding. In 2019, CAPE was combined with the Center for Army Leadership to form the Center for the Army Profession and Leadership (https://capl.army.mil/).

10 Kilner (2016).

11 Wood (2014).

12 Alison Hills observes that "the practice of exchanging reasons and the motivation to find a justification that could not be reasonably rejected by others is clearly morally very important" (2012, 199).

13 Wood (2016, ch. 1).

14 Driver (2015, 34).

15 Ibid.

16 Richard Schoonhoven takes the point further, stating that if soldiers "can never (be in a position to) know whether their country's wars are unjust, it is hard to see how or why ordinary citizens – the rest of us – should be better situated epistemologically" (2010, 115).

17 I take the first two of these conditions for justified deference from Driver (2015, 35).

18 Driver (2015, 36).

19 This difference between moral and epistemic deference is part of what fuels the academic debate on the possibility of moral experts. See Ryle (1957), Singer (1972), and Driver (2013), among several others (whom they helpfully cite).

20 This notion of trusteeship, therefore, seems to support selective conscientious objection, a proposal that would allow soldiers (or citizens facing a draft) to refuse participation in a specific war, instead of the current policy of only allowing the rejection of all wars. I acknowledge the possible connection but do not explore it further here.

21 Shanks Kaurin (2020, 31).

22 Orend (2013, 175).

23 Walzer (2015, 38–40).

24 Litz et al. (2009, 705).

25 Wood (2014). It is important to note that Dundas' concern does not seem irrational in principle; in fact, there is something commendable in his refusal to simply insist on the justice of the war no matter the devastation he witnessed. I bring this up to further reinforce the limited nature of moral deference proposed above.

26 MacKenzie (2017, 12). MacKenzie takes the term "remote intimacy" from Gusterson (2016).

27 There is an irony in the US military's simultaneous efforts at training soldiers and developing technologically advanced equipment: even as it attempts to limit the autonomy of its human recruits by settling for moral testimony instead of understanding, it is trying to increase the autonomy of its machines. It seems to seek a greater "machine-likeness" in its humans and "human-likeness" in its machines (MacKenzie 2017, 18). Both efforts are practically and morally concerning and underscore the importance of research focused on optimizing the human-machine interface.

28 Shay (1994, 116).

29 Shay (2002, 2014); Litz et al. (2009); Wilson (2014); Winright and Jeschke (2015); Sherman (2015); Wood (2016); Meagher and Pryer (2018).

30 Litz et al. (2009, 699; emphasis in original).

31 Wilson (2014, 61).

32 Verkamp (1993, 72–85); see also Shay (2002, 168–169) and Winright and Jeschke (2015, 174–175).

33 Litz et al. (2009, 703).

34 Verkamp (1993, 32–34). The Eastern Orthodox Church maintains this practice in the present day.

35 This section, therefore, draws on ideas associated with a Christian worldview and doctrine. It is unapologetic in two senses: first, I do not try to apologize for engaging in ideas rooted in Christian thought (they are a prevalent part of our world and academic discourse); second, I do not try to advocate, in some evangelistic way, for the exclusively Christian version of the ideas ("apologize" in the theological sense). I simply want to examine the help with moral injury that notions like penance and atonement offer. Is it possible to do this – to engage Christian ideas not as propaganda, but also not as fiction?

36 Winright and Jeschke (2015, 187).

37 To reinforce this point, Stump spells the term as "at onement" throughout her first chapter (2018, 3–38). Stump cites Linda Radzik's research to define atonement as "setting at one;" see Radzik (2009, ch. 1.2).

38 Stump (2018, 7).

39 Both types of moral injury may generate other forms of discord. Trust in one's leadership, for example, may be broken, as well as trust in oneself. Here, I identify only the discord appearing later in this section.

40 Litz et al. (2009, 701).

41 Aquinas (1485, I-II q.86 a.1 and 2).

42 Stump (2018, 57).

43 My thanks to Eleonore Stump for this distinction and the phrase "stain on one's life."

44 Hallie (1979).

45 Ibid., xvi, xviii.
46 Ibid., xix.
47 Stump (2018, 54).
48 Ibid., 364.
49 James Dubik in his foreword to Sherman (2015).
50 Stump (2018, 364).
51 Litz et al. (2009, 701).
52 The quotation is from the latter organization's website: <https://www.mis-sioncontinues.org/about/>.
53 Stump (2018, 375; italics added).
54 Ibid., 379.
55 Ibid., 373.
56 Shay (2002, 169); Litz et al. (2009, 703); Wood (2016, ch. 14).
57 Stump (2018, 374).
58 Many scholars of moral injury emphasize the need for community: Shay (1994, 2002); Litz et al. (2009); Wilson (2014); Sherman (2015); Wood (2016).
59 As cited by Zahavi (2014, 140).
60 Litz et al. (2009, 699).
61 Similarly, for soldiers overcoming moral injury through spiritual or religious practices, empathy with a benevolent deity can generate a compelling sense of one's own value, offsetting self-doubt and self-condemnation. This empathetic moment may help explain studies showing the relevance of spirituality to morally injured soldiers; see, for example, Litz et al. (2009, 703); or Howsepian (2016).
62 Litz et al. (2009, 703; italics in original).
63 Wilson (2014, 68).
64 Shay (1994, 4); this theme recurs in Litz et al. (2009, 703); Sherman (2015, 18–21); Wood (2016, ch. 15); and others.
65 Litz et al. (2009, 704).
66 Shay (2002, 168).

Index

Note: Page numbers followed by "n" denote endnotes.

guilt of 22–23; John Lee 14–15;
moral testimony, clarifications
95–100; need for atonement
101–107; Nik Rudolph 13–14;
overcoming 100–110; preventing
92–100; recovery from 90, 110; risk
of 10–22; Romeo Dallaire 12–13;
Shay's CIB recipient 11–12; Shay's
seasoned soldier 13; tragic betrayal
15–17; tragic right-doing 17–21;
tragic self-betrayal 21–22; types 16,
101–102, 104, 105, 107
moral insensitivity 20
moral labor 97
moral residue 19–21, 103–105,
106, 109
Mullen, Michael 60
My Lai 5

naïve fallibility 47, 55n85
naïve realism 46
narrative competency 39
narrative theory 34, 38–40, 42
nonhumanization 66, 67, 81

operational planning 7
other-oriented perspective-taking
35, 42

peace 12, 27, 29, 56, 58–61, 65, 71–73,
82, 110, 111; negative 59, 60, 65,
71, 82; positive 60, 71
post-traumatic stress disorder
(PTSD) 10, 30n39, 100
proportionality 2, 76
propositional memory 107

recognition respect 42
reconstructive empathy 40
reenactive empathy 40
reflective morality 57, 58
reflective suffering 24
Reserve Officer Training Corps
(ROTC) program 94
right intention 2, 56–62, 72–74,
82, 83, 85, 86; neglect of 56–61;
reviving 62–74
Rommel, Erwin 98
Rudolph, Nik 13–14, 17, 18,
91, 105

rule-based approach to morality
57–58
Rwanda 12

Scales, Robert 5
Scheler, Max 36, 41
Schoonhoven, Richard 113n16
Schutz, Alfred 36
self-loathing 22, 24
self-oriented perspective-taking
36, 63
Shay, Jonathan 4, 11–13, 15, 17,
18, 20, 65, 69, 70, 93, 102, 105,
110; *Achilles in Vietnam: Combat
Trauma and the Undoing of
Character* 4
Sherman, Nancy 5
simulation theory 33, 35–37, 39, 40
Smith, Adam 33
Smith, Joel 41
social distance 66
social perception 39
Stein, Edith 36, 107
Stueber, Karsten 40, 44
Stump, Eleonore 22–23, 44, 45, 49,
90, 101, 103, 105–107
subhumanization 66
Sylvester, Christine 4
sympathy 9, 32, 33

technical problems 78
theoretical inference 34
theory-theory 33–37, 39–41
Thompson, Hugh 5
tragic betrayal 15–17, 23
tragic right-doing 17–21
tragic self-betrayal 21–22, 102
transgression 18, 21, 22, 103
Trojans 69
trolley problem 18, 19
Tutsi 12

US Army doctrine 1, 7, 10
US policy-making 6

Verkamp, Bernard 101
Vietnam War 59, 82

de Waal, Frans 49
Waldman, Matt 6, 7, 9

Printed in the USA
CPSIA information can be obtained
at www.ICGtesting.com
LVHW081933071123
763306LV00006B/156

9 781032 163413